CRITICAL APPRAISALS SERIES
General Editor: John Fletcher

GÜNTER GRASS

The Writer in a Pluralist Society

MICHAEL HOLLINGTON

Marion Boyars
LONDON · BOSTON

for Barbara and Barnaby

Published in Great Britain and the United States in 1980
by Marion Boyars Publishers Ltd
18 Brewer Street, London W1R 4AS
and Marion Boyars Publishers Inc.
99 Main Street, Salem, New Hampshire 03079

Australian distribution by Thomas C. Lothian
4–12 Tattersalls Lane, Melbourne, Victoria 3000

© Michael Hollington 1980

British Library Cataloguing in Publication Data
Hollington, Michael
Günter Grass.—(Critical appraisals series).
1. Grass, Günter—Criticism and interpretation
I. Series
833′.9′14   PT2613.R338Z
ISBN 0–7145–2678–9 cloth edition
Library of Congress Catalog Card Number 79–42857

Printed in Great Britain by Robert MacLehose & Co. Ltd
Printers to the University of Glasgow

CONTENTS

ACKNOWLEDGEMENTS

Acknowledgements are due to Hermann Luchterhand Verlag, for permission to quote from the writings of Günter Grass; to Martin Secker & Warburg Ltd., for the British Commonwealth excluding Canada and to Harcourt Brace Jovanovich Inc., for the U.S.A. and Canada for permission to quote from the English translations of Grass's works, as listed in the bibliography; to Pantheon Books for permission to quote from *After Hitler*, by Jürgen Neven-DuMont; to Holt, Rinehart & Winston for permission to quote from *A Social History of the Third Reich* by Richard Grunberger.

Discussion with friends and colleagues helped me considerably during the writing of this book. I should like to mention only a few: John Fletcher for encouragement, Michael Parkinson for help with the rural background, Walter Bachem for help with close reading, Rodney Foster for information about the German critical scene. For the chapter on *The Flounder* I should like to thank Maria and Karlheinz Diedrich and Ulf Lie.

FOREWORD

Günter Grass is still in his early fifties, but many of his writings are already established as contemporary classics. A recent bibliographer,[1] without having to be unduly systematic, manages to list over 750 critical writings on his work; a recent critic[2] calls for a scholarly biography, an edition of letters, and critical editions of the already published works. Grass provides material for school curricula and examinations in many countries; he is a favourite of literary journalists and chat-show compères. Possibly the safest bet in those literary circles in which such things are of significance is that Grass, at some precocious age, will be the recipient of the Nobel Prize for Literature.

Such achievements in the eyes of some seem to entail a loss of esteem amongst those who form the most alert and progressive literary audience. To become a classic in our time (as Max Frisch has said of the case of Brecht) may involve being condemned to ineffectuality. Grass, who in the early sixties represented to the intelligentsia of the left the 'active conscience of Germany' (the phrase is George Steiner's), is now widely mistrusted as a treacherous establishment liberal. For Gertrude Cepl-Kaufmann, representing the new generation of radical intellectuals in Germany, he is no longer of contemporary relevance.

Two reasons for this decline in Grass's prestige as a critic of contemporary German society seem to stand out. The first is specific to Germany – the emergence of a post-war generation for whom Grass's preoccupation, the German guilt accumulated in the Nazi period, is a dead issue. Their focus is upon the inadequacies and abuses of the present governmental system of the Federal Republic; liberal democracy has for them no value in itself, as it had for Grass and his generation, brought up in the Nazi period. The second is more general and has to do with a very widespread deterioration, in Western Europe at least, of the vitality of the liberal humanist tradition. Grass, with his vigorous and consistent adherence to the ideals of the Enlightenment and their fragmentary continuation in the Weimar Republic, begins to look distinctly old-fashioned in the late seventies, its intellectual climate dominated by Marxism and structuralism.

From a contemporary perspective Grass now seems a writer whose essential roots lie in the humanist existentialism of the fifties and early sixties. The idea of the essential isolation of the human individual in an absurd, contingent world without necessary meaning is, *pace* Oskar's ironic dismissal of it at the beginning of *The Tin Drum*, of central importance in Grass's work. As with a writer like Iris Murdoch, Grass's existentialism carries a strong moral (for Marxists, moralistic) flavour: the realization of the irreducibility of phenomena, their complexity and absurdity, is a positively valued recognition of the nature of historical reality. Within the context of German history, his work also carries a recognizably existentialist emphasis upon the necessity of responsibility and commitment in the face of such an apprehension of reality.

At the same time, it can also be shown that Grass as a writer relates to very much older ideas and traditions. The distinctive need of German writing, in the period at which Grass began to work, was to connect with its own powerful modernist tradition, and beyond that with its own highly imaginative tradition of fantastic realism, both entirely obliterated during the Nazi period. Grass writes within the tradition of the grotesque, mingling fantastic and realistic, horrific and comic elements of fiction as a rhetorical strategy designed to involve the reader in questioning his preconceived notions of the normal and the real.

In adopting this approach I have been indebted to classical accounts of the grotesque in literature, notably to Mikhail Bakhtin, and also to the work of one German critic of Grass in particular, Georg Just.[3] This is a work for the general reader, and my use of Just is necessarily of a simplified kind, and does not enter into many theoretical considerations; nonetheless, it seems to me that the essential theoretical issues raised by Grass's work concern the problems encountered by the reader as he attempts to negotiate deceptive ironic strategies in the tradition of Sterne and Jean Paul. The neglect of this aspect of Grass's work is in my view what renders so much of the Grass criticism arbitrary and decidedly unhelpful. My book, then, is an attempt to present Grass as an essentially comic writer within the liberal humanist tradition as it encounters our pluralist world and is affected by existentialism, and to aid English-speaking readers in appreciating the techniques and purposes of Grass's irony. I have attempted to include discussion of all of Grass's published writings, but inevitably my attention is unevenly distributed, with the chief focus falling on Grass's output as a novelist. I have used Ralph Manheim's translations of Grass's writings wherever these are available: on occasions, particularly in the case of Grass's political writings, I have had to make my own translations, a task which increases my respect for Manheim's work.

NOTES

1. George Everett, *A Select Bibliography of Günter Grass* (New York: Burt Franklin, 1974).
2. Gertrude Cepl-Kaufmann, *Günter Grass: Eine Analyse des Gesamtwerkes unter dem Aspekt von Literatur und Politik* (Kronberg/Ts: Scriptor Verlag, 1975).
3. Georg Just, *Darstellung und Appell in der 'Blechtrommel' von Günter Grass. Darstellungsästhetik versus Wirkungsästhetik.* (Frankfurt am Main: Athenäeum Verlag, 1972).

BIOGRAPHICAL INTRODUCTION
Keeping the Wound Open

Günter Grass, like many writers in this century, lives in exile from his birthplace and imaginative sources. Langfuhr, the suburb of Danzig (Gdansk) in which he was born and brought up is now Polish Wrzeszcz – 'who can pronounce that?' asks Oskar in *The Tin Drum* (p. 411). Joyce's project, in *Ulysses*, 'to give a picture of Dublin so complete that if the city one day suddenly disappeared from the face of the earth it could be reconstructed out of my book,'[1] closely parallels a major impulse of Grass's writing: to memorialize the lost world of pre-war Danzig. Hans Magnus Enzensberger described Grass's first novel as 'a saga of the submerged Free City of Danzig, a poetic salvation from oblivion of that little world in which Germans and Poles, Jews and Cassubians lived together.'[2] Grass himself has declared in conversation[3] that he has at last come to a satisfying formulation of the function of the writer, which he delivers in *From the Diary of a Snail*: 'A writer . . . is someone who writes against the passage of time . . .' (p. 124).

Unlike Joyce, Grass's relationship to the lost city is fundamentally affectionate and even nostalgic. The critical skepsis that characterizes his work dissolves momentarily when the image of Danzig in the memory is invoked: 'Doubt will agree with me: it was lovely in Danzig. The clouds entirely different. The snow much whiter. Boat trips to Kalte Herberge by way of Fischerbabke. Towers and steeples big and little: zinc-green and brick-red. The two timber-frame warehouses on Mausegasse, where silent in their overcoats aged

1

Jews went on hoping . . .' (p. 123). But the aged Jews disrupt
the picturesque idyll, serving as a reminder that the loss of
Danzig is no accident, but the historical consequence of
criminal policies and a war conducted to achieve their aims.
One of Grass's essential subjects as a novelist is the responsibility that individual members of a society bear for historical
events: it can be said that his art, and later his political
activity, are a working out of his own sense of responsibility
for recent German history. It is worthwhile, then, devoting
some attention to Grass's life and career in the context of the
Danzig background and Germany's post-war history.

Günter Grass was born on 16 October 1927. At that date
the Free City of Danzig was in the seventh year of its existence, and Weimar Germany was enjoying a short-lived period
of prosperity and stability. From 1793 until 1920, Danzig had
been part of the province of West Prussia (except during the
Napoleonic period); the Treaty of Versailles after World War
I, seeking to provide Poland with access to the sea through
the only significant port on that part of the Baltic coast,
severed Danzig from the German Reich and recreated it as a
Free City under the protection of the League of Nations. The
idea was to resurrect the golden age of Danzig prior to 1793,
when as a free Hanseatic port Danzig had served Poland
amicably and to mutual advantage as an outlet for trade.[4]
This arrangement was patently artificial; it satisfied none of
the parties concerned, least of all the German majority in
Danzig, who remained solidly in favour of reintegration with
the Reich throughout the inter-war period. Their 'plight' was
to be the pretext of Hitler's invasion of Poland in 1939.

And yet Danzig, as capital of the province of West Prussia
under the Reich, had suffered a gradual decline in prosperity
and prestige during the nineteenth century. Under Bismarck,
Germany underwent astonishingly rapid industrial development, and yet Danzig emerged with only one industry:
shipbuilding. Meanwhile, in comparison with other German
ports (Hamburg in particular) its share of trade failed to

expand.[5] Grass's suburban birthplace Langfuhr was the product of the development of the shipyards; such pre-war
glamour as it possessed consisted in its function as the base
of the Black Hussars and as the residence of their commander
the German Crown Prince[6] (but in *Dog Years* the barracks
have become the headquarters of the police). Otherwise its
population consisted chiefly of industrial families with many
children, and of small tradesmen catering to their needs.
Amongst these latter was Grass's father; like Matzerath, in
The Tin Drum, he kept a grocer's shop.

The world of Langfuhr in the inter-war years is described
at length in *Dog Years*:

> . . . with its kitchen gardens, drill grounds, drainage
> fields, slightly sloping cemeteries, shipyards, athletic
> fields, and military compounds, . . . Langfuhr, which
> harboured roughly 72,000 registered inhabitants . . .
> possessed three churches and a chapel, four high schools,
> a vocational and home-economics school, at all times
> too few elementary schools, but a brewery with Aktien
> Pond and icehouse . . . derived prestige from the Baltic
> Chocolate Factory, the municipal airfield, the railroad
> station, the celebrated Engineering School, two movie
> houses of unequal size, a car barn, the always over-
> crowded Stadium, and a burned-out synagogue. . . .
> (p. 337).

It is evidently provincial, philistine, materialistic, ugly. Its
petit-bourgeois inhabitants, struggling to survive as the
depression hit Germany, were prime targets for Hitler, who
projected himself as the saviour of the 'little man' of Germany.
The depression had a particularly severe effect on Danzig,
which had to deal not only with the contraction of world
trade but also with intense competition from the new port of
Gdynia, constructed by Poland because of their mistrust of
the Free City arrangement. The Nazi party, as a result of the
depression, achieved earlier and greater success in Danzig

than in the Reich itself; already in 1930 it held the balance of power in the Danzig senate, and in May 1933 won a bare absolute electoral majority in free elections, something that Hitler was never to achieve in the Reich. As elsewhere, it was in the suburbs and rural areas of the Free City territory, rather than in Danzig itself, that the Nazis found their chief support.[7]

'And I grew up, was reared between the Holy Ghost and Hitler's photograph.' (*Poems of Günter Grass*, p. 80). The Nazi party laid immense stress on its 'youth policy'; the young, freshly indoctrinated at school and at Hitler Youth meetings, were to convert and replace the old, corrupted by democracy. Grass was five when Hitler came to power; inevitably he went through the Party's standard stages of indoctrination. At the age of ten, boys became *Pimpfs* (Hitler cubs), and at fourteen, fully-fledged members of the Hitler Youth. Before the age of ten, the mere 'child' hardly mattered: official jargon held that 'the term "child" describes the non-uniformed creature who has never participated in a group meeting or a route march.'[8]

It is hardly surprising, then, that the theme of the perversion of childhood plays such a prominent part in Grass's work. Familial roles were reversed: children had to assume political responsibility, guiding and possibly denouncing backsliding elders, while parents reverted to childish, irresponsible roles as the Führer took over his position as father of the nation. Grass confides to his children in a recent novel that he was 'sometimes older (then) than I'll soon be . . .' (*From the Diary of a Snail*, p. 69). Boys were encouraged to develop strongly masculine roles and, girls were made to conform to a myth of submissive femininity: ten-year-olds learnt to use guns, to compete fiercely in physical sports, to behave aggressively and ruthlessly in the eradication of enemies. 'When I was fifteen, I wanted, in thoughts, words, and works, to murder my father with my Hitler Youth dagger.' (p. 69).

Grass seems to have been an exceptionally gifted child, who

drew, painted and read voraciously and 'absolutely' (p. 69), in faithful imitation of his indoctrinators. At the age of thirteen, spurred on by a competition sponsored by the Nazi school-magazine *Hilf mit!* he began to write a novel called *The Cassubians*.[9] It seems safe to speculate that this work would have been a reflection of the Nazi *Blubo* cult (*Blut und Boden*, meaning blood and soil) with its standard recipes for an idealization of a peasantry engaged in pagan earth-worship, rooted in a local rural community and fiercely antagonistic to the modern city. The 'holy ghost' opposite Hitler in Grass's family was Cassubia, the homeland of Grass's mother: Cassubian themes, superstitions and land-scape have a considerable significance for Grass's imagination.

The Cassubians are an old Slavonic race inhabiting the hilly country to the west of Danzig (contained in the Polish Corridor during the inter-war years), speaking a language separate from Polish yet closely related to it. Grass's mother was of Cassubian origin; the region from which she came is described in the opening chapter of *The Tin Drum*. Marrying a Danzig German, she reflects the drift away from the land to the city, and also perhaps the ambiguous position of the Cassubians, neither German nor Polish, oscillating according to expedience (like Anton Stomma in *From the Diary of a Snail*) between two masters. They are a peasant race with a culture that still manages to cling on to survival, pious, thrifty, superstitious. Their folklore is not concerned with heroic exploits but rather with the dealings of trickster figures with a capacity for survival, 'whose weapons in the struggle for existence are ruses and prudence.'[10] Such qualities, we shall see, go into the conception of Oskar Matzerath in *The Tin Drum*, but we may also imagine how they enabled Grass's mother to survive and adapt in the *petit-bourgeois* world of Langfuhr.

'. . . sand, all clammy/for making castles, until my child-hood grail/gothically towered and collapsed.' (*Poems of*

Günter Grass, p. 78). This image from the poem 'Kleckerburg' suggests the extent of the shock that occurred to disrupt Grass's secure childhood world, with its reference points in the Hitler Youth and the Cassubian countryside. The shock was delayed until about 1943, the early war years being a good deal more sheltered for most German families than for most people in Britain. Grass volunteered as an anti-aircraft auxiliary at the age of fifteen, and became a soldier at the age of sixteen. His was the generation of Manfred Gregor's novel *Die Brücke* (*The Bridge*, also a significant film), made up of boys of sixteen or younger called up at the end of the war to fill the gaps caused by the enormous manpower losses on the Russian front and to defend Hitler and Berlin from the advances of the Russian Army; incongruously, these children were forbidden to enter cinemas unaccompanied by adults. Education, under such circumstances, was the first thing to suffer; a Danzig contemporary of Grass describes 'field-classes' for anti-aircraft auxiliaries:

> The front was coming closer and closer, the teachers came out to us and gave us classes right on our gun emplacements. Our school principal came out there too. He taught Latin. We were reading something or other of Livy and all of a sudden he said: 'We've got to hold together now, just like the old Romans!' He tried to teach us the civic spirit that had welded the Romans together. He was a very convinced Nazi and a very hard man. Besides, we had a biology teacher. He was a theology student who had gone wrong. He dragged everything connected with the Church through the mud. He knew all his bible quotations by heart. He could start talking about a radish and end up with some bible quotation that he'd reel off with a cynical twist; for instance: 'Let us make here three tabernacles, one for me and one for thee and one for the Jew Elias.'[11]

Such edification failed to sustain the morale of the generation of the 'burnt children'. The following years of Grass's life comprise the crucial experiences of disillusionment and betrayal. First, the shattering experience of actual combat. 'I grew up with special communiqués in my ear,' hearing endless reports of victory and superhuman bravery, Grass recounts in one of his political speeches (*Über das Selbstverständliche (On the Self Evident)*, p. 142) – but on the first day of action thirty of his comrades, half an entire company, were killed 'without so much as seeing an enemy.' (*Speak Out*, p. 56). Thereafter Grass himself was wounded at Cottbus on the day of Hitler's last birthday and taken into a prisoners' camp at Fürstenfeldbrück in Bavaria by American soldiers. Early in 1946 he was discharged in the Rhineland, to begin the process of adjustment to shattered ideals:

> At the age of eighteen I was discharged from an American POW camp: it was only then that I became an adult – or rather that I gradually began to realize what, behind a smokescreen of martial music and irredentist bilge, *they* had done to my youth. It was only then that I began to find out – the full horror was not revealed to me until years later – what unthinkable crimes had been committed in the name of the future of my generation. (*Speak Out*, p. 55).

The most important thing about this stage of Grass's development seems to be that he did not resume the normal middle-class educational progression from *Abitur* to university; instead, he became nomadic, working first as a farmhand in the Rhineland, then in a potash-mine near Hildesheim, then as a stonemason's apprentice in Düsseldorf (compare the wanderings of Walter Matern in *Dog Years*). At one point, presumably during the Hildesheim period in 1946, he began to try to catch up on his secondary school work, but it is highly significant that he quickly abandoned this attempt because of the way in which history was taught: 'As soon as the history teacher started on about the Ems Telegram, I'd had enough.'[12] History was evidently still about great men, nationalism, war.

Grass now came into close contact with working men and women – the potash miners, the stonemasons, and through his sister in Düsseldorf, the nurses who figure importantly in his novels (Grass says he was well looked after in every respect by the nurses in Düsseldorf). He became conscious of class differences and antagonism: the stonemason to whom he was apprenticed in Düsseldorf (an old man called Singer who had worked on the Bismarck monument) was mistrustful of his secondary school origins, and of his desire to go to art school. Above all, it is in these years that Grass's associations with the Social Democratic Party begin.

The first stage of Grass's political re-education probably began in the prison-camp. In his 1967 speech in Israel he recounts a story of this period about two young men of his own generation, one the survivor of a concentration camp, the other of service in the German army in the Ardennes, and of their mutual antipathy towards an Austrian-Jewish historian who accompanied the American troops as 'a kind of cultural attaché . . .' (Speak Out, p. 93). This man, Mautler, is the hero of the anecdote; he attempts to instil values stemming from the Enlightenment that Grass himself later espouses in his public political role, reason, tolerance and patient reformism, into boys possessed by fanatical aggressions and hatreds. In the Hildesheim potash-mine in 1946 Grass detects the same constellation of forces: moderation on the one hand, extremism of the Left or of the Right (habitually equated in Grass's thinking) on the other. Grass listened to the political discussions of the miners, 'my ears still full of Hitler Youth reveilles, every Sunday morning swearing oaths to the flag, to the blood and of course to the soil as well.' . . . 'Little harmless old Nazis' and 'embittered communists' seem to have found grounds of agreement with each other, at least when they sided in opposition to their common enemy the Social

Democrats. It was the former Social Democratic voters among the workers who gained Grass's respect:

> As a 'burnt child', I sided cautiously with my tight-lipped Social Democrats, who waffled neither about the thousand year Reich nor about world revolution, but who already then in 1946 had dispatched the debris of ideological ballast up to the pithead together with the rest of their produce and who were more progressive than the party leaders. . . . I'm grateful to those skeptical old socialists, battered from left and right, worn out in the heat and fumes, for teaching me how to live without some goal in the clouds, without symbols or decorations or the pasteboard models of heroic comrades. (*Über das Selbstverständliche*, p. 59).

In this period too, early in 1947, as political life began to resurrect itself in Germany, Grass went to his first political meeting, to hear the old Social Democrat Kurt Schumacher.

Out of these experiences grew an antipathy to idealists with abstract theories and ideologies, a preference for pluralist skeptics of the non-ideological Left; Grass's work as a writer and as a political activist takes this position as its primary premise. For Grass experience is always more significant than theory, in art or in politics: 'A twenty-four year old electro-welder is miles ahead of a student of sociology at that age in his experience of life or political insight.' (*Günter Grass: Dokumente zur politischen Wirkung* (*Documents on Grass's political impact*), p. 132). Such assertions alienate the Marxist left, in their denial of the unity of theory and praxis. They are, I think, best understood in the context of the psychology of a man whose formal education was decisively interrupted, and the ideology that sustained it fundamentally discredited: having given himself wholeheartedly to an absolute as a child, and been so brutally betrayed by it, Grass cannot bring himself to accept any alternative ideologies. He thinks of the most important part of his education as gained outside of formal institutions, through experience, observation, self-imposed reading and study. There is an interesting description of him in the mid-fifties following his own course of reading. 'A systematic autodidact, who takes what he needs, gets good nourishment from it, digests it, puts it to use.'[13] 'From eighteen on, I tried to survey that corral and discovered how intricately subdivided it is and how reason and intellect are seldom neighbours: the greater the intelligence, the more devastatingly its stupidity can run wild.' (*From the Dairy of a Snail*, p. 69).

Yet after 1948 Grass did enrol as a student at the Düsseldorf Academy of Art and studied sculpture under Sepp Mages and Otto Pankok, earning money at night by playing in a jazz-band, and also beginning to write poems. 'I spent quite a long time living very little but only writing; I was a storehouse for dispersed fragments, also for duly entered losses.' (p. 69). Grass's development as a writer in the post-war years was inevitably slow; he spent a great deal of time gathering material, experimenting with forms, working out a relation-ship to the past. Starting as a poet, he then began to write plays and only when these proved unsuccessful did he turn to the novel; there is a story that some of Grass's poems were shown to Gottfried Benn (then the grand old man of the German lyric) by mutual friends in 1953, and that Benn thought they showed talent, but advised the author to turn to prose instead. Grass made notes in the summer of that year towards what was to become *The Tin Drum*, but felt himself as yet unconfident in the dimensions of the novel; nonetheless Grass says of his move to Berlin in 1953 (where he continued his studies at the Academy of Art under Karl Hartung) that 'I came as a writer.'[14]

During the period of the middle and late fifties Grass began gradually to make his mark as a writer. In 1954 he married Anna Schwarz, a ballet student in Berlin from a prosperous Swiss family, and it was she who is supposed to have taken the step that first led to Grass's being noticed by the literary establishment. (The marriage has since ended in divorce, and Grass remarried in May 1979.) She sent in some poems to a competition organized by the South West German Radio, in 1955; one of them, 'Lilien aus Schlaf' ('Lilies of Sleep') won him third prize. These poems were then published in *Akzente*, the magazine of the 'Gruppe 47', a group of writers formed in 1947 in an attempt to nurture a post-war renaissance of German literature.[15] *Akzente* in 1955 knew very little about Grass: he is simply (and inaccurately) described as 'Günter Grass from Berlin' in the biographical notes, and the prize-winning poems are accompanied with the information that 'Karl Schwedhelm of South German Radio brought these poems to our attention.'

The 'Gruppe 47' was decisive in launching Grass's career as a writer, and also of very considerable importance in the formation of his artistic and intellectual temperament. One of its leading figures, Walter Höllerer, heard Grass read poems in Berlin in May 1955 at one of the group's meetings, decided to sponsor him, published some of his poems in a collection called *Transit* and helped to foster Grass's first volume of poems, *Die Vorzüge der Windhühner* (*The Advantages of Windfowl*) published by Luchterhand in the autumn of 1956. Meanwhile Grass had gone to live in Paris, where his wife wanted to continue her ballet studies, and it was here that *The Tin Drum* was begun: the bulk of it was written at 111 Avenue d'Italie. The turning-point came in 1958: on his last twenty marks (according to one perhaps romanticized version)[16] Grass went to the 'Gruppe 47' congress, held that year in the Allgäu in Southern Germany. He read the first two chapters of *The Tin Drum* and won the group's prize of 5000 DM; the prize enabled him to make a return visit to Poland (he went there again in 1959). At least as significant, however, is the fact that the prize began a process of institutionalization as the representative of a resurrected German cultural tradition. Grass continues to speak admiringly of the 'Gruppe 47' as the embodiment of enlightenment values: 'In the Gruppe 47 there was certainly always a critical atmosphere, but also always one that was either tolerant or saw itself compelled to be tolerant . . . .'[17]

The Tin Drum was published in 1959; it brought its author instant celebrity or notoriety, which together reportedly brought in 400,000 DM in the course of four years. The two other novels in the Danzig trilogy followed in 1961 and 1963, a second volume of poems *Gleisdreieck* appeared in 1960 and the remainder of Grass's early plays were published before 1961. Looking back, we can see this period of the late fifties and early sixties as encompassing an extraordinary burst of creative energy which Grass has not since been able to recapture. Since the publication of *Dog Years* in 1963 Grass has published four novels, one volume of poems and two plays (one of them a dramatized version of *Local Anaesthetic*).

Any attempt to explain this fact must give an account of Grass's active involvement in politics in the sixties and early seventies. The first evidence of this involvement came in 1961, when he helped Willy Brandt's campaign to become Chancellor by providing gags and quotations for some of Brandt's speeches, but the origins of Grass's political engagement must be sought before that. The apparently absurdist and apolitical poems and plays of the fifties are full of oblique reference to political and social realities, above all to the experience of the refugee. The central image is that of the house, of threats to its solidity, of the uprooting of its inhabitants. In his later political speeches one can gain a glimpse of how Grass watched events in the fifties for signs of a widening gap between East and West: the Adenauer years between 1949 and 1963, in which the 'politics of strength' were practised, are punctuated for him with betrayals of the possibilities for reunification or reconciliation with the East. The Workers' Uprising in East Berlin in 1953 – Grass is scornful of the candles placed in West German windows on the 17th June, in lieu of more positive response; the re-armament of West Germany in 1955; the building of the

Berlin wall – these events seem to mark the periods of post-war history for Grass, and render the loss of Danzig permanent and irrevocable (see *Günter Grass: Dokumente zur politischen Wirkung*, p. 182).

Also of considerable importance in explaining Grass's conversion to political activism is his close friendship with and admiration for Willy Brandt. The portrait of Brandt in *From the Diary of a Snail* makes clear that what Grass admires is his skepsis, proneness to melancholy, uncertainty about taking power – the guarantee of his political integrity by comparison with the CDU opposition, who regard power as their natural right. Brandt is also a representative of tolerance, in particular in his attitude towards his son Peter who belonged to the violent radical Left in the disturbances of the late sixties; he is again the antidote to fanatical hatreds and prejudices (p. 154; clearly the themes of *Local Anaesthetic* show through). And perhaps most interesting for the student of Grass as a writer is the fact that Grass regards Brandt as a representative of the intellectuals in exile during the Nazi period and hence as the upholder of the progressive tradition of German Social Democracy. Grass was incensed that Adenauer, in August 1961, at the time of the Berlin wall crisis, saw fit to refer to Brandt's illegitimate birth and emigration from Germany during the war (cudgels that have since formed a standard part of the CDU's electoral tactics, often to Brandt's considerable personal distress): ' . . . in 1961 began the wholesale denigration of Brandt and the emigration – things that affected me very directly (and here literature comes into it again), because I knew what the literature of the emigration had meant to me.'[18]

Mann and Brecht, the two great (antagonistic) central figures of emigration literature, have had a marked effect upon Grass's writing: Mann, upon the instinctive and constant use of parody, particularly of the *Bildungsroman*; Brecht, upon Grass's attempt to work out and demonstrate his own variety of epic theatre in *The Plebeians Rehearse the Uprising*; both, upon Grass's attempt to re-establish the modernist tradition. Just as in the post-war years Grass had to work out a relation to the past on the personal and political level, so the problem for the writers of his generation was to discover literary roots: 'We who were brought up under National Socialism had to work out afresh all that we'd never had, for instance the relationship to an interrupted literary tradition, to expressionism, etc. . . .'[19] The predicament can be seen to have its advantages as well as disadvantages, compared for instance with the situation in England in the fifties, where the institutionalized heroes of Modernism (Yeats, Eliot, Joyce) provoked the conservative reaction of the 'angry young men.' Grass may have looked like a German 'angry young man' when *The Tin Drum* appeared, but in reality his artistic and political attitudes are fundamentally dissimilar: he shows a constant awareness of the radical political meaning of modernist experiment in art (which the Nazis also recognized by suppressing it) and a desire to apply and develop it. Grass reacted with rage when Ludwig Erhard (then the German Chancellor) used the language of Goebbels to attack the dramatist Rolf Hochhuth as a 'degenerate artist': 'Paul Klee and Max Beckmann, Alban Berg and Kurt Weill, Alfred Döblin and Else Lasker-Schüler were driven out of this country with the phrase you parrot with a redoubled irresponsibility, Mr. Erhard.' (*Über das Selbstverständliche*, p. 40).

'What kind of insight is to be gained through loss,' asks Grass in a newspaper article of 1970 (*Der Bürger und seine Stimme* (*The Citizen and his Voice*), p. 155). The permanent loss of Danzig, the temporary loss of a literary and intellectual tradition entail for Grass a consciousness of the significance and responsibilty of the artist in society that in Britain may seem more Victorian than modern. Initially, *The Tin Drum* was condemned for its nihilism or cynicism; in the seventies, it is more likely to be criticized for its ponderous moral artistic standpoint. Grass is conscious that his writing adopts

a *via negativa* in its method of representing contemporary
society – that is to say, it suggests a morality by implying its
absence from things as they are. This is apparent for instance
in a declaration Grass made as part of a legal action against
someone who had accused his writing of being pornographic
(the case was lost): 'It is astonishing that one has to keep on
pointing out how firmly established the role of the blas-
phemer is, both in the New Testament and the Old. I
remember the wicked thief at the crucifixion; it is only
through his counter-position that the position of the good
thief is made clear.' (*Günter Grass: Dokumente zur politischen
Wirkung*, p. 315). And Grass goes on to claim in the same
testimony that this function belongs not only to critical
modernists but to a vigorous European satiric tradition that
includes Petronius, Boccaccio, Rabelais and Jean Paul:
'Allow me to say, that as a writer, I am thoroughly conscious
of the tradition of European literature; and if I seek to defend
myself against slander, I do so not only on my account, but
for the sake of the great narrative tradition to which I am so
much indebted.'

Such passages read ambiguously: the 'high seriousness'
claimed for the comic writer in our time reflects a very positive and rare confidence in art, but there is also a self-
consciousness, unctuous at times, concerning the writer's
official public status. Grass has achieved international fame
since 1959, and in Germany he is a media-hero packaging
sometimes platitudinous exhortations about the moral and
political responsibilities of the individual citizen. Grass
claims in *From the Diary of a Snail* to hold his public image
at an ironic distance (of Fame, allegorized as a boarder in the
Grass household, he asserts 'I often rent him out at a small
fee for receptions and garden parties' – (p. 70)) but I think one
can only be certain of this in Grass's political writings where
the language is correspondingly fresh and critically conscious
of cliché.

Grass's most habitual language of reference for his political

activism is existentialist. He describes it as a way of authen-
ticating the positions adopted in his literary work:

> I don't regard it as a sacrifice, but as a valid necessity for
> me, and as an activity that puts me in question, some-
> thing that literature, because of the benefits or draw-
> backs of fame, hasn't been able to offer me in the last
> few years. . . .
>
> It's cost me a lot of time, if you want to draw up an
> account or balance it, but it's brought me a lot of new
> experiences and put me in question, involved me in risks,
> at the cost even of stylistic spontaneity and narrative
> facility: but I'll buy that, it's part of the game.[20]

Direct political intervention entails for Grass the assumption
of responsibility, and more essentially still, of guilt for
historical events. He is scornful of writers who express their
political commitment only through the medium of art; they
are in 'bad faith', allowing themselves to escape into formalist
defences against the open-endedness of reality: 'A writer who
does not participate in the catastrophes of reality – for often
enough participation means guilt – can construct his own
catastrophes and in the last chapter provides the catharsis for
them at cost price.' (*Speak Out*, p. 45). The commercial
metaphor, so characteristic of Grass's political writings,
reflecting perhaps the early experience of a grocer's shop,
stands as the index of authenticity.

Continually for Grass action involves guilt. Electioneering
leaves the stains of guilt: 'The election campaign has left spots
on my paper' (p. 36), as, at the opening of *The Tin Drum*,
Oskar's commitment of his memories to paper involves the
sullying of the virgin page. In *From the Diary of a Snail* Grass
expresses guilt for the death of August, the suicide who
attends one of his political meetings; elsewhere, he focuses
upon guilt for the Prague invasion of 1967 and the deaths of
students in the Berlin street-riots of 1968. The assumption of
responsibility for everyday disasters is designed as an

exemplary model of a full assumption of a historic guilt that Grass believes post-war West German society to have more or less evaded. As a public speaker, it is a theme on which he is often impressive: 'When I was nineteen, I began to have an inkling of the guilt our people had knowingly and unknowingly accumulated, of the burden of responsibility which my generation and the next would have to bear. I began to work, to study and to sharpen my distrust of a *petit bourgeois* society which was once more assuming such an air of innocence.' (*Speak Out*, p. 56).

Such is the rationale Grass provides for his participation on behalf of Willy Brandt and the Social Democrats in three successive elections, 1965, 1969, and 1971. What began as a private 'Voters' Initiative' campaign – and incurred the deep mistrust of many local Social Democrat candidates in the 1965 election – led to Grass's acceptance as a quasi-official party intellectual and personal adviser to Willy Brandt. Grass was offered numerous safe parliamentary seats, advocated as Mayor of Berlin, rumoured as the imminent recipient of ministerial responsibility, particularly in the field of Overseas Development. Grass accompanied Willy Brandt on official visits to Poland and Israel, and took some part in the negotiations with the Soviet Union over the recognition of borders in Eastern Europe; but his commitment to political life has gone no further. Since Willy Brandt's resignation in 1974, Grass has continued to campaign on behalf of the Social Democratic party (see *Der Bürger und seine Stimme*, p. 265), but does not seem able to summon up the same fervour on behalf of the government of Helmut Schmidt. It seems that the most intense period of Grass's political activism is now past, and his artistic activity thoroughly reinvigorated.

For much of the time since 1953 Günter Grass has lived and worked in Berlin. Geographically, it is nearer to Danzig than any other part of West Germany. It offers 'perhaps the only group of people in Germany which developed a political

18   GÜNTER GRASS

sense since the war,'[21] and a daily reminder of the consequences of history, in a situation where a visa is required
to get, as it were, from Charing Cross to Leicester Square.
In February 1968 students and other young people on the
streets of Berlin were seriously injured in clashes with the
police. Grass's response, when these events were no longer
in the forefront of public attention a couple of weeks later,
typifies his sense of responsibility towards contemporary
history: 'And those things that really happened can be
stylized away, tomorrow even, before they repeat themselves,
as some kind of burdensome nightmare. I want to warn
against this time-honoured means of dealing with the past;
I prefer, myself, to keep the wound open.' (*Günter Grass:
Dokumente zur politischen Wirkung*, pp. 96–7).

NOTES

1. Frank Budgen, *James Joyce and the Making of 'Ulysses'*
   (London: Oxford University Press, 1972), p. 69.
2. Hans Magnus Enzenberger, 'Wilhelm Meister auf Blech
   getrommelt', *Einzelheiten* (Frankfurt am Main: Suhrkamp
   Verlag, 1962), reprinted in Gert Loschütz, *Von Buch zu
   Buch - Günter Grass in der Kritik* (Neuwied and Berlin:
   Hermann Luchterhand Verlag, 1968), p. 11.
3. See Gertrude Cepl-Kaufmann, op. cit., p. 305.
4. See Christoph M. Kimmich, *The Free City: Danzig and
   German Foreign Policy 1919–34* (New Haven, Conn: Yale
   University Press, 1968), p. 9.
5. See Ian F. D. Morrow, *The Peace Settlement in The German-
   Polish Borderlands*, (London: Oxford University Press, 1936),
   p. 33.
6. Hans Leo Leonhardt, *The Nazi Conquest of Danzig* (Chicago:
   Chicago University Press, 1942), p. 16.
7. Leonhardt, pp. 58–60.
8. Richard Grunberger, *A Social History of the Third Reich*
   (Harmondsworth: Penguin Books 1974), p. 353.

9. See *Der Spiegel* 4/9/63 for this and much useful biographical information.

10. Friedrich Lorentz, Adam Fischer and Tadeusz Lehr-Splawinski, *The Cassubian Civilization* (London: Faber & Faber, 1935), p. 172.

11. Jürgen Neven-DuMont, *After Hitler: Report from a West German City* (Harmondsworth: Penguin Books, 1974), p. 127.

12. *Der Spiegel* 4/9/63, p. 66. The Ems Telegram was Bismarck's ploy for avoiding responsibility for declaring the Franco-Prussian war.

13. Theodor Wieser, *Günter Grass* (Neuwied and Berlin: Hermann Luchterhand Verlag, 1968), pp. 7–8.

14. Gertrude Cepl-Kaufmann, p. 34, quoting from 'Writers in Berlin. Three-way discussion with Walter Höllerer and Walter Hasenclever', *Atlantik* 12, 1965.

15. For some useful information on 'Gruppe 47' see W. G. Cunliffe, *Günter Grass* (New York: Twayne Publishers, 1969), pp. x–xii.

16. Hugo Loetscher, *DU* (Zurich, June, 1960); reprinted in Loschütz, p. 191.

17. Heinz Ludwig Arnold, 'Gespräch mit Günter Grass', *Text und Kritik* 1/1a (October 1971), p. 5.

18. ibid., p. 20.

19. ibid., p. 3.

20. ibid., pp. 14, 21.

21. Quoted in Gertrude Cepl-Kaufmann, p. 34.

THE DANZIG TRILOGY I
The Tin Drum

Since 1964[1] Grass has repeatedly asked that the three novels
on which his fame and reputation as a writer chiefly rest –
The Tin Drum, *Cat and Mouse* and *Dog Years* – be considered
as components of a 'Danzig trilogy'; the arrangement has
now been formalized by the Luchterhand reissue of the novels
under that title. It is not easy to assess the significance to be
attached to this grouping. That the novels have important
features in common – Danzig as a subject, overlapping
characters, events, themes – is self-evident; but it is my view
that the search for closer thematic or metaphoric links
between them can be misleading.[2] They embody a conception
of art that is antipathetic to formal patterning, which seeks
instead to render a view of reality as tangled, multiple and
incomplete. The 'matter of Danzig', as it emerges in these
works, is inexhaustible, not to be confined within the space of
three acts.

In the three following chapters I have, therefore, chosen to
deal with each novel as an independent unit rather than as
part of an overall structure. Nonetheless, I hope that certain
recurrent issues come clearly into focus. The chief of these is
the relation of the present and the past. All three novels are
about the rescue of the past from oblivion; the act of narration itself carries the function of memorializing that which for
more and less reputable reasons threatens to pass out of
collective memory. 'Keeping the wound open' implies also the
direct involvement of the reader in the resurrection of what
lies buried in his memory; the utilization of the structure of

the novel, and the reader's memory-processes as he reads, is
part of Grass's strategy for realizing this aim. The prolix,
baroque structure of *The Tin Drum* and *Dog Years* in particular, designed to perform this function, places those works
squarely within a witty anti-classical tradition of formal
experiment in the novel.

> And what of this new book the whole world makes such
> a rout about? – Oh, 'tis out of all plumb, my lord – quite
> an irregular thing! – not one of the angles at the four
> corners was a right angle. – I had my rule and compasses,
> etc., my Lord, in my pocket.[3]

The conception of *The Tin Drum* developed slowly, over a
period of several years. 'The first notes began in the summer
of 1953. In February, 1959, the manuscript was completed.'
Even before 1953, Grass was working with themes that
essentially prefigure those of the novel: in 1950/1 he went on a
trip to France and wrote a cycle of poems called *Der Säulen-
heilige* (*The Saint on the Column*), which has never been
published. The poems concern a young stonemason (Grass's
occupation in the Düsseldorf period), who withdraws from
the world, builds himself a stone column, has his mother
bring him food, and describes the world as it appears from
this vantage point. 'At a later date, Oskar became the reverse
of a saint on a column. It developed that the man on the
column was too static for me to have him speak in prose, and
for that reason Oskar came down from the column. He did
not stay at normal height but came a little closer still to the
earth, and then had a point of view the opposite of that of the
saint on the column.'[4]
Despite the change in the conception, the dwarf Oskar
Matzerath and the St. Simon Stylites figure have two
important things in common. Firstly, they are both removed
from the everyday world, and describe it from a standpoint of
detachment and non-involvement. Oskar writes his novel
from his bed in a mental hospital, resenting intrusions from

the outside world upon his securely withdrawn seclusion; likewise up until the end of the war, he takes refuge in his size and ambiguous childishness as a means of evading involvement in the adult world. Secondly, both standpoints imply optical distortions of 'normal' reality: the saint on the column sees the world reduced in size, with distances foreshortened, the dwarf sees the world enlarged and magnified, with distances and dimensions exaggerated. It is this latter point that I shall develop first, for it helps to explain the significant presence of the grotesque, not only in *The Tin Drum*, but in Grass's work as a whole.

Traces of the St. Simon Stylites conception survive in *The Tin Drum* itself, for Oskar is addicted, not only to holes and hideaways, but also to heights. In the apartment house where his parents live, he is a frequent visitor to Meyn, the occupant of the attic: from there he sees the monotonous routines of surburban existence, as in a labyrinth of courtyards carpet-beating housewives on Tuesdays and Fridays are multiplied a hundredfold (p. 92). From there he graduates to the Stockturm towering above Danzig, and later in the scene of the Dusters' trial to a diving platform where the whole of the world is laid out before his feet. Again its monotony is apparent – a tram conductor in Finland is breaking eggs into a frying-pan while a woman in Panama is burning the milk; 'historic' events are made to look insignificant, as the huge elephants of Mountbatten's Burma campaign are taken in with the same glance as a pair of aircraft carriers 'done up to look like Gothic cathedrals' sinking in the Pacific, their planes hovering 'helplessly and quite allegorically like angels in mid-air.' (p. 377). Like God, the amateur cameraman 'who each Sunday snaps us from above, at an unfortunate angle that makes for hideous foreshortening . . .'. (p. 45) Oskar looks down from his heights upon a distorted picture of the world.

Conversely, from his dwarf-perspective Oskar perceives a world magnified to an unmanageable size. On his first day at school, Oskar is unable to reach the water-fountain made for normal-size children, is led by his mother 'up monumental stairs hewn for giants' (a satiric glance, perhaps, at the superman proportions of Nazi public buildings), and is unable to see anything but sky out of the school windows (pp. 73–4). At coffee in a smart Danzig coffee-house with his fellow-midgets Bebra and Roswitha, Oskar is struck by the disproportion between the company of dwarfs and the waiter who serves them, 'like a tower in evening clothes.' (p. 165).

Such visual distortions are a hallmark of grotesque art. From Rabelais onwards, the tradition of the grotesque (transmitted in England through Swift, Sterne, Dickens, and later Joyce) frequently employs a perspective that monstrously enlarges or diminishes objects of everyday perception, 'making strange' that which is thought to be familiar. In Sterne, for instance, the narrator of *Tristram Shandy* looks at the world on occasions as if through a microscope, seeing spermatozoa as 'homunculi' composed of 'skin, hair, fat, flesh, veins, arteries, ligaments, nerves, cartilages, bones, marrow, brains, glands, genitals, humours, and articulations' in a comically literal version of Aquinas.[5] In Dickens the world of the city is frequently seen through the eyes of a child, enlarged, out of proportion and frightening. The grotesque in literature owes a great deal to the visual arts;[6] it has its modern origins in the Mannerist artists of the later Renaissance who used the newly discovered 'grotteschi' of antiquity (fantastical cave-paintings combining human and animal forms) as the basis of a reaction against the humanist-inspired rules of proportion adopted in the High Renaissance. Classical art implies symmetrical balance, harmonious proportion, and the limitation of formal elements; mannerist, and later grotesque art, formal imbalance (*Tristram Shandy* devotes much of its attention to events preceding the narrator's birth), distortion and excess.

In *The Tin Drum*, Oskar is highly aware of the fact that his physical appearance and view of the world conflict with the

canons of classical taste. The embodiment of the classical
ideal in the novel is Goethe, one of Oskar's twin mentors:
Oskar knows that 'if you, Oskar, had lived and drummed at his
time, Goethe would have thought you unnatural, would have
condemned you as an incarnation of anti-nature . . .' (p. 86).
Oskar and Herbert Truczinski appraise the Niobe statue with
classicist eyes; lengthwise, she conforms to Dürer's propor-
tional system, but as to width, she has the grotesque proportions of a Dutch witch (pp. 186–7). Ideals of proportion are
mocked at the funeral of Oskar's mother: he discovers the
perfect classical image of stasis in the shape of her coffin: 'Is
there any other form in this world so admirably suited to the
proportions of the human body?' (p. 159).

Grotesque representations of distorted forms also challenge
our conventional notions of 'normal' reality. The world of
everyday reality is 'made strange'; the strange and fantastical
is presented in a matter-of-fact way as if it were commonplace.
Grass claims to have written *The Tin Drum* in conscious
opposition to the Kafkaesque imitations of German writers of
the fifties; nonetheless, the influence of Kafka is felt in the
casual introduction of the fantastical into a predominantly
realist setting that characterizes *The Tin Drum*. Kafka's
Metamorphosis opens with the calm notation of a fantastical
event; Oskar's announcement of his supernatural faculties is
equally prosaic: 'I may as well come right out with it: I was
one of those clair-audient infants whose mental development
is completed at birth and after that merely needs a certain
amount of filling in.' (p. 42). Such strategies are designed to
confuse and disorient the reader, pre-empting his responses:
Oskar presents 'clair-audient infants' as if they were a
common category of language. The reader's unfamiliarity
with any such category, tends to provoke puzzlement: 'what
am I to make of this?'

Readers are likely to suspect metaphor, symbol, or folklore. The fantastic elements in grotesque writers are frequently
drawn from fairy-tale or myth. Gogol started his career

writing folktales, purveying to the St. Petersburg taste for Ukrainian local colour; when he turned his attention to the city itself, he used the folk-material he had accumulated to highlight the equally fantastical reality of the Russian civil service. Dickens' work draws frequently on fairy-tale motifs, most notably perhaps in *Dombey and Son*, where the child's unnatural educational force-feeding makes Paul a modern version of the monstrous elf-changelings of folk legend.

This particular example brings us close to the case of Oskar. It seems quite likely that Grass's conception has popular imagery in mind, especially since Cassubian folklore is steeped in stories about dwarfs:

> The belief in the dwarfs or goblins (*krosnjeta*, among the Cassubians in German Pomerania *undererczkji*, 'gnomes') is still very much alive. These are small beings, about a foot in height, of human shape, and of male and female sex, who lead a perfectly human life: they celebrate weddings and christenings, have names, and die. . . . They are ruled by a king, who wears a golden crown on his head, and are fond of merry conviviality, music and the dance. They live more than a thousand years, but have no souls . . .
>
> The vindictiveness of the *krosnjeta* is much to be feared. If they are driven out of a house by curiosity, the former luck turns into misfortune. . . .
>
> The *krosnjeta* are extremely dangerous to an unbaptized child, which they like to exchange for one of their own, in order to make it their king or queen, according to the belief of the Cassubians. In order to protect the children against being exchanged in this way, the Catholic Cassubians put rosaries or scapulars round their necks, while the Protestants put a hymn-book in their cradles, or a decoction of consecrated herbs is mixed with their bath-water. Should the exchange nevertheless take place, the mother is sometimes made aware of the fact by the

senile, ugly features of the changeling; then she must beat it till the blood runs, whereupon she will get her own child back, though likewise in an injured condition. If she fails to notice the exchange, the child will always remain undersized. . . . People of short statue are often called changelings.[8]

Many features of *The Tin Drum* seem to reflect this material: Oskar's supernatural powers, his vindictiveness towards the house of Matzerath, the feeling of community amongst the dwarfs in the novel, their timelessness, the superstitious fears of the grown-ups about Oskar's relations with his fellow-midgets, etc.

Yet the identification of a possible source in folklore for Oskar's psychic powers does little to dispel the reader's perplexity. In fairy-tales, there is no first person narrative; the strangeness of the fairy-world is acknowledged as such, and presented in an imaginatively distanced way.[9] The strategy of the fantastic as it is used in grotesque art is quite different: there it is embedded in a realistic texture, designed to create familiarity and to promote identification with its characters and setting. Likewise the operation of two equally important functioning opposites in grotesque art, the comic and the horrific; comic devices – like the frequent use of a stylistic disproportion between formal rhetoric and ludicrously mundane subject-matter – distance us from the situation presented (we tend to laugh only at that which does not affect us directly and immediately), while horrific details (which normally affect us very directly) are simultaneously present. In grotesque art, the distancing effects of comic and fairy-tale elements and the immediacy of realist and horrific techniques are combined in disturbing tension: we laugh at what would normally be painful, and we are forced to concede the reality of the conventionally fabulous.

One might take as a paradigm the extraordinary world of Mr Venus in *Our Mutual Friend*. Mr Venus's shop is a quite 'normal' taxidermist's, yet the optical perspective – extreme chiaroscuro, and hence the focusing of the eye upon parcels of light that fragment the scene – succeeds in making it strange and frightening. Objects that rationally can only be dead and still – limbs, stuffed animals, bottled embryos – acquire in the gloom an irrational tendency to spring to life: '. . . Mr Wegg gradually acquires an imperfect notion that over against him on the chimney-piece is a Hindoo baby in a bottle, curved up with his big head tucked under him, as though he would instantly throw a summersault if the bottle were large enough.' Stylistic imbalance generates comedy – Venus refers to the skeletons as 'the lovely trophies of my art', and puffs his work to the purchaser of a stuffed canary with 'There's animation! On a twig, making up his mind to hop!' – but the laughter is uneasy: the boy departs together with his canary and a missing tooth in his change, and counters Venus's rage with: 'I don't want none of your teeth, I've got enough of my own.'[10] The tooth is not stylized and distanced, as it would be in purely comic art; it might be the boy's, or Mr Venus's, or our own.

Similar techniques are employed in *The Tin Drum* in the chapter 'Disinfectant.' The characteristic grotesque method of character portrayal in the novel – most of the minor characters are caricatures in the style of Sterne's Uncle Toby, reduced to a very limited number of attributes which are normally eccentric 'hobby-horses' (Vincent Bronski is obsessed with the Queen of Poland, Mrs Truczinski with her husband's death, the nightclub owner Schmuh with the periodic slaughter of a dozen small birds) – is not abandoned for the former inmate of Treblinka Fajngold. Fajngold's hobby-horses are the persistent spraying of disinfectant and conversations with his dead relatives, murdered in the concentration camp. Oskar is ill with the effects of growing, and Fajngold's obsessions are refracted through the optic of Oskar's feverish hallucinations; the nightmarish reality of Treblinka is presented at a double distance. Comic techniques

B

are employed: Fajngold's obsessive disinfecting is rendered ludicrous through the mechanically repeated verbs ('he rubbed . . . sprayed . . . and powdered', 'he sprayed, powdered and rubbed', 'he had sprayed, strewn and sprinkled'), and the stylized rhetoric is carried right into the description of Treblinka itself (' . . . *alles was aus den Öfen herauskam, alles was in die Öfen hineinwollte*'/'. . . all that came out of the ovens and all who were about to go in' – Grass's grim irony simultaneously dehumanizes the victims of the gas-chambers and attributes volition to them). Yet minute realist detail counteracts the stylization, placing us in a firm, recognizable historical context (Fajngold must barter rolled oats and synthetic honey for his disinfectant, the world of Treblinka is rendered with painstaking exactitude down to the precise Yiddish spelling of the inmates' names), breaking in upon the reader's detachment. The oscillation between stylization and horror prohibits conventionalized responses that might either mythologize or rationalize away the reality of Treblinka.

The passage thus suggests how grotesque art may be used as the vehicle of radical moral and social criticism: Mr Venus's shop in *Our Mutual Friend* is itself a fractured image of the trafficking in human bodies that characterizes the social and economic practices portrayed in the novel. Grotesque writing creates a dynamic relationship between text and reader, the latter being denied any unambiguous or preconceived reactions. The aesthetics of classicism, consisting in the mimetic representation of a completed, static segment of reality, are in sharp contrast to those of grotesque art, which challenge our received notions of the real, the ordered and the natural. As the profoundest writer on the grotesque, Mikhail Bakhtin, puts it:

> Actually the grotesque liberates men from all the forms of inhuman necessity that direct the prevailing concept of the world. This concept is uncrowned by the grotesque and reduced to the relative and limited. Necessity, in

every concept which prevails at any time, is always
one-piece, serious, unconditional, and indisputable. But
historically the idea of necessity is relative and variable.
The principle of laughter and the carnival spirit on which
grotesque is based destroys this limited seriousness and
all pretense of an extratemporal meaning and unconditional value of necessity. It frees human consciousness, thought and imagination for new potentialities.[11]

Or nearer home, there is the testimony of Brecht: 'Seriousness
as a way of life is a little discredited at the moment; because
the most serious things there have ever been are Hitler and Co.
Hitler's one of your serious murderers, because murder is a
very serious business. The Buddha, by contrast, has a sense of
fun.'[12]

The dynamic relation of text and reader that characterizes
The Tin Drum is apparent in the novel's first sentence:
'Granted: I am an inmate of a mental hospital; my keeper is
watching me, he never lets me out of his sight; there's a
peephole in the door, and my keeper's eye is the shade of
brown that can never see through a blue-eyed type like me.'
(*The Tin Drum*, p. 11). The first word presupposes an audience,
one that is made to be a participant in a conversation, that
has made an accusation that the writer attempts to rebut. The
implied accusation is sarcastically philistine and the narrator
seems to be defending himself by saying: 'All right, I may be a
looney, but . . .' Only there is no 'but'; the narrator doesn't
complete his sentence by means of a conventionally correct
syntax, but seems to get side-tracked by the mention of his
keeper, forcing the reader to participate once more in
completing the sense of the sentence. Is the disordered syntax
evidence that he is indeed mad? Is he a paranoid insisting
on his invulnerability to brown-eyed persecutors? Is he
an ex-Nazi priding himself on his Aryan superiority?
The with holding of information to satisfy the reader's

curiosity compels the reader into active collusion with the narrator.[13]

Grass's aim in *The Tin Drum* is 'to put the reader in question' about his past, his involvement in and responsibility for the crimes committed by the National Socialists. The audience in mind is specifically that of the German Federal Republic, an affluent society basking in the German 'economic miracle' and ostensibly quite recovered from its traumatic past. That society is essentially pluralistic: journalism, television and radio provide an abundance of conflicting ideas, images and information about the present and the past. History is experienced as something fictional, acted out in front of television cameras by a cast of figures remote in time and space, available to instant replay. The question of the relation between individual actions and historic consequences is buried by abstractions: 'Naive consciousness thinks of the everyday world as a natural atmosphere or as a known, familiar reality, whilst history appears to it as a transcendent reality . . . the division of life into the everyday and the historical is experienced as fated.'[14]

The writer, the creator of deliberate fictions, is thus beset by severe difficulties in the portrayal of contemporary history. His very medium is suspect, catering to more or to less sophisticated evasions: fictions are used or abused as an escape from the greyness of everyday life, as a 'heightening' of reality, or as the repositories of symbolic abstractions. Grass's approach in *The Tin Drum* is to use the fictiveness of fictions as an exemplum; by involving the reader, by making him aware that he collaborates with Oskar in the making of the novel, he attempts to awaken a critical consciousness of the process of evasion. The approach to contemporary reality is thus indirect, a negative process of uncovering self-deceptions through strategic irony.

Thus Oskar is constantly concerned about his reader's response to his narrative. He is anxious to please wherever possible: he wants to provide suspense in Chapter Two by withholding the name of the city that is to be his setting (Danzig!) and then divulging it unexpectedly (pp. 21, 28). He wants to avoid digressions, invoking 'our Father in Heaven' at the beginning of Chapter Four to guard him from his 'penchant for the tortuous and labyrinthine' (p. 45); he wants to spare us from the boredom of descriptions of Danzig's roof-tops (p. 99) which illustrated calendars can do a great deal better. He appreciates the reader's thirst for explanatory information, a common technique being the anticipation of the reader's questions (e.g. pp. 317–8, 548), which Oskar always attempts to answer directly: 'What business took me abroad? I won't beat about the bush . . .' (p. 312); where he feels the need to leave gaps in order to advance his narrative, he is polite and apologetic: 'Perhaps, since I am burning to announce the beginning of my own existence, I may be permitted to leave the family raft of the Wrankas . . .' (p. 25). He is conscious of the readers' appetite for variety, dislike of excessive repetition: 'I still had my voice, which is of no use to you now that you have heard all about my triumphs with glass and is probably beginning to bore the lovers of novelty among you . . .' (p. 355). As the novel progresses, he increasingly provides *aide-memoires* in the form of catalogues of former events or images in the novel, in case we've forgotten them; Oskar encourages our memories by distributing compliments when we recognize echoes of previous chapters, 'As you have doubtless noticed by now, I had always, under tables, been given to the easiest kind of meditation . . .' (p. 207); '. . . it is up to you to recognize the sighs and saints' names that were uttered in '99 when my grandmother sat in the rain . . .' (p. 210); 'I am referring, as the most attentive among you will have noted, to my teacher and master Bebra . . .' (p. 300). He tries to avoid frighteningly vivid realist effects, such as the one he fears for the description of Greff's winter dips in the ice: 'Oskar is not trying to send winter shudders running down your spine. In view of the climate, he prefers to make a long story short . . .' (p. 287).

Clearly, these devices are ironically intended: the concern to spare us from boredom and repetition strikes at a consumer-psychology; the fear of chilling our spines with descriptions of winter landscapes archly suggests that we may perhaps be immune to some of the real horrors in the book. Yet a good deal of the irony looks innocuous enough on the surface, a function of Oskar's consciousness that we expect dwarfs to be entertaining. Some of the jokes at our expense stem from music-hall: 'Do you know *Parsifal*? I don't know it very well either.' (p. 466). Oskar likes to tease us for our lasciviousness, knowing very well that it's the girl on Lankes's lap that interests us more than Lankes himself: 'Let me speak with the painter first and describe the Muse afterwards.' (p. 462), and that we're dying to hear about the man who gets sexually aroused by stepping on his girlfriend's toe: 'Later – this Oskar relates only to satisfy the curious amongst you – Mr Vollmer . . . did come to our Cellar.' (p. 519). The reader's materialistic values are satirized – 'Why so many words about a cheap carpet which might at most have had a certain barter value before the currency reform? The question is justified.' (pp. 504–5) – along with any misplaced condescension we might feel about Oskar's bourgeois origins: 'You will say: how limited the world to which this young man was reduced for his education!' (p. 300).

Yet Oskar's insinuated camaraderie with his readership masks fiercer challenges to complacency. These emerge first, perhaps, in the chapter where Oskar attends a Nazi Sunday parade: 'Did it have to be the Maiwiese? you may ask. . . . even at the risk of being thought a fellow traveller I must admit that I preferred the doings on the Maiwiese to the repressed eroticism of the scout meetings.' (p. 112). The attitudes imputed to the reader are designed to disconcert, not only Oskar's ex-Nazi admirers, but any facile dispensers of the 'fellow-travelling' cliché. When Oskar has described how he disrupted the meeting, he again challenges hypocrisy: 'That word "resistance" has become very fashionable. We

hear of the "spirit of resistance", of "resistance circles".
There is even talk of an "inward resistance", a "psychic
emigration". . . . Yes, I did all that. But does it make me, as I
lie in this mental hospital, a Resistance Fighter? I must answer
in the negative . . .' (p. 119) Oskar's asceticism aims at
provoking the reader to examine the quality of the 'resistance'
with which he may have dressed up his own past. Elsewhere,
Oskar's guilt for having betrayed his parents drifts dis-
concertingly towards generalization: 'But on days when an
importunate feeling of guilt, which nothing can dispel, sits on
the very pillows of my hospital bed, I tend, like everyone else,
to make allowances for my ignorance – the ignorance which
came into style in those years and which even today quite a
few of our citizens wear like a jaunty and oh, so becoming
little hat.' (pp. 241–242).

Such passages now seem moralistic – certainly they give the
lie to the pervasive conception of *The Tin Drum* as a cynical,
nihilistic book. The wit is generally sharper, however,
constructing sudden pitfalls for the reader, on the 'innocent'
topic of fizz-powder, for instance; 'Who started up with the
fizz powder? The old old quarrel between lovers. I say Maria
started it. . . . She left the question open and the most she
would say, if pressed, was: "The fizz powder started it." Of
course everyone will agree with Maria.' (p. 264). The view so
swiftly thrust upon us challenges a recognition of our readi-
ness to transfer responsibility to some other 'they' or 'it'.
Equally sudden is the deflation of pretension in some of the
passages of deceptively dense symbolism:

> For quite some time, absorbing and sleep-dispelling
> images passed before Oskar's eyes. For all the dense
> darkness between the far walls and the blacked-out
> windows, blond nurses bent over to examine Herbert's
> scarred back, from Leo Schugger's white rumpled shirt
> arose – what else would you expect – a sea gull, which
> flew until it dashed itself to pieces against a cemetery

wall, which instantly took on a freshly whitewashed
look. And so on. (p. 270).

A separate come-uppance is reserved for symbol-hunters of a
Freudian (or Rankian) persuasion. 'You've guessed it no
doubt: Oskar's aim is to get back to the umbilical cord; that
is the sole purpose behind this whole vast verbal effort and
my only reason for dwelling on Herbert Truczinski's scars.'
(p. 173).

The sarcastic hostility towards symbolic interpretation is
basic to the conception of the novel. Symbolism is regarded
as a reductive and schematic abstraction of the complexity of
reality – as if the 'whole vast verbal effort' could be reduced
to one 'sole purpose.' Metaphors are regarded as irresponsible
evasions or childish word-games: '. . . I had always, under
tables, been given to the easiest kind of meditation: I made
comparisons.' (p. 207), or, in the context of the reader's
expectation of symbolic and synthetic heightening of the
prosaic and everyday:

> Nowadays every young man who forges a little cheque,
> joins the Foreign Legion, and spins a few yarns when he
> gets home a few years later, tends to be regarded as a
> modern Ulysses. Maybe on his way home our young man
> gets into the wrong train which takes him to Oberhausen
> instead of Frankfurt, and has some sort of experience on
> the way – why not? – and the moment he reaches home,
> he begins to bandy mythological names about: Circe,
> Penelope, Telemachus (p. 339).

Hence the constant use in *The Tin Drum* of mock-metaphor
and mock-simile, designed to call attention to their own
arbitrariness and incongruity. The most interesting of these
connect the trivialities of everyday life to the grand events of
history: thus Oskar's glass-shattering voice is compared to
Hitler's 'miracle weapons' that were supposed to settle the
war (p. 365, the translation rather missing the point of '*jetzt*

nenne ich sie, die Wunderwaffe'), the difficulties of two
Chinese Lesbians in achieving satisfactory physical connec-
tion are compared to the problems of reunifying the two
German states (p. 461), and Max Schmeling's parachuting
injury during the invasion of Crete with Maria's fall from the
ladder (p. 291). The most extended example is the simile
comparing Oskar's difficulties in making love to the filthy
Mrs Greff and the German advance on Moscow:

> I hope I shall be forgiven for drawing a parallel between
> the muddy triumphs of Army Group Centre and my own
> triumphs in the impassable and equally muddy terrain
> of Mrs Lina Greff. Just as tanks and trucks bogged down
> on the approaches to Moscow, so I too bogged down;
> just as the wheels went on spinning, churning up the mud
> of Russia, so I kept on trying – I feel justified in saying
> that I churned the Greffian mud into a foaming lather –
> but neither on the approaches to Moscow nor in the
> Greff bedroom was any ground gained (pp. 298–9).

The satiric effectiveness of this absurd metaphor is multiple,
taking in amongst its targets the self-glorification of the *petit-
bourgeois*, the euphemisms of Nazi propaganda ('triumphs',
like the successful 'front-shortenings' [retreats] of p. 324,
being a perversion of language), and the familiar German
denial of responsibility for Hitler's crimes.

It is through parody that the novel attempts to activate
critical awareness of the potentialities of language for the
blurring and veiling of reality. Stylistically *The Tin Drum* is a
constant mimicry of clichés, stereotypes and pseudo-
profundities, springing their nullity upon us, as the poetic
travelogue sentence describing Reims illustrates: 'Sickened by
humanity, the stone menagerie of the world-famous cathedral
spewed water and more water on the cobblestones round
about, which is a way of saying that it rained all day in Reims
even at night.' (p. 322). There is space to consider only two
of these, the piece of *Blubo* with which the novel opens and

the detective-thriller with which it closes, since these have
strategic importance in guiding our responses.

Chapter One exorcises Grass's fifteen-year-old attempts to
romanticize Cassubia for the consumption of Nazi schools.
It contains the standard props of the Nazi rural idyll – the
earth-mother, the emphasis on being rooted to the land, in the
race-consciousness – all in parodic form. The month is
October (at the end of a century too), the weather cold, the
landscape grey and monotonous, the costumes drab. Harsh
realities intrude – it is difficult to keep warm, the fire hard to
ignite and keep going, the food primitive. The grandmother's
'race-consciousness' is a peasant cunning that easily outwits
the caricatured Prussian gendarmes, themselves a Laurel and
Hardy parody *'dick und dünn'* (fat and thin) – Laurel and
Hardy in Germany are *'Dick und Doof'* (Fat and Foolish).
Her 'blood-rootedness' to the soil is farcically represented in
Koljaiczek's penis. The grandmother's role in the novel is
complex and demands further discussion, but the parodies in
Chapter One discourage the reader from indulgence in
nostalgic pastoral myth as a flight from contemporary
reality.

In the closing chapter Oskar is conscious of the need to
satisfy the consumer demand for stereotyped literary endings
with a bang not a whimper, and offers two equally parodic
alternatives: the figure thirty, with its nice circular symbolic
pomposity, neatly rounding out the original fall at his third
birthday (cf. p. 145), or the excitement of a murder hunt.
Oskar stage-manages, wishing to provide a suitably dramatic
point of capture, yet his imagination stretches no further than
Orly airport ('an interesting place'/*'besonders pikant und
originell'* – p. 573). Suitable mystification is provided: did
Oskar do the deed, or was it a classic lovers' triangle? That
other mystery, the black witch, fraught with symbolic
significance for some critics, seems to me the appropriate
parody-image of the demonization of guilt and responsibility
that the novel so squarely confronts.

Beginnings and endings round off literary fictions, encapsulating them against the contingencies of reality: here both are subjected to a radically skeptical critique. The episodic structure of *The Tin Drum* – identified by Kayser as characteristic of grotesque form[15] – militates against tight formal coherence; the three-part division of the novel (pre-war, wartime, post-war) is modelled on history[16] not numerology or symbolic pattern. Through techniques learnt from Sterne and Jean Paul, Grass attempts to dispel our comfortable assumptions about the correspondence between the shape of fictions and the shape of history. To understand that ' "convention", and "automatized" perception of reality . . . the evil in itself, in as much as it hinders insight into the possibility of changing the world and thus robs actual change of its essential prerequisite'[17] is the target of Grass's witty rhetorical strategies seems the essential basis of an adequate reading of *The Tin Drum*.

According to Nazi racial mythology, there were young, vital races and old, decrepit ones (like the French); the Germans, predictably enough, counted as 'more childlike than any other nation'.[18] The treatment of the 'little man' and his relation to history in *The Tin Drum* ironically bears this out. The SA men who vandalize Markus's shop during the *Kristallnacht* of 1938 find themselves at home: '. . . there, in their characteristic way, they were playing with the toys' (p. 197); ('characteristic' translates *'eindeutig'*/ 'unambiguous', in significant contrast to Oskar). Out at the seaside on Good Friday, Matzerath and Jan Bronski hop from stone to stone, 'gambolling like schoolboys.' (p. 143). The intrusions of history do nothing to disturb their 'innocent' childishness: Jan Bronski plays skat as the Polish post office falls and a world war beings; at the bombardment of Danzig Matzerath rushes up and down the stairs watching the city on fire, 'bewildered as a child who can't make up his mind whether to go on believing in Santa Claus . . .' (p. 384). Nothing changes after the eclipse of the

Nazis, for Oskar's post-war fame as a pop star depends on his ability to reactivate childhood: 'they gave vent to their pleasure . . . burbling and babbling like three-year-olds.' (p. 546).

This debased childishness is the expression of a flight from adult responsibilities. Characteristically, the *petit bourgeois* adults of Langfuhr are shown in their private lives allocating blame to someone else, or to an abstraction like 'fate'. Oskar's glass-shattering voice tests bourgeois conscience with his incisions into shop-windows, and uncovers its shuffling evasiveness: 'Suddenly there was a hole in the glass and by the time I had half-way recovered from my flight and was three blocks away, I discovered to my consternation that I was illegally harbouring a pair of wonderful calfskin gloves, very expensive I'm sure, in my coat pocket.' (p. 124). Matzerath wants to make it clear to his wife that he's not responsible for her Good Friday trauma: 'If only we'd never gone out there. Can't you forget it Agnes? I didn't do it on purpose.' (p. 155). Conversely, in this parody of a quarrelsome marriage, Agnes exonerates herself of any responsibility for Oskar's fall (though she was engaged in musical flirtation at the time), branding Matzerath as a 'murderer' (p. 58). She thus forges a potent weapon for marital strife, to be resurrected at will; when Matzerath is wounded by it, she too feels guilty, and they join forces, declaring their joint blamelessness, comforting themselves with the fiction that Oskar is a 'cross they had to bear, a cruel and no doubt irrevocable fate, a trial that had been visited on them, it was impossible to see why.' (p. 81). The latent political attitudes here are subtly conveyed in cliché; Nazi propaganda rationalized race-hatred with the slogan 'the Jews are the cross we must bear.'

Compromising action is undertaken by the 'little men' of Langfuhr only covertly and discreetly, to avoid unpleasant consequences. Shame is an important motivating factor, dictating conformity with accepted public standards; that lack of 'civil courage' which Bismarck felt to be charac-

teristically German is much in evidence in *The Tin Drum*.
Dückerhoff sets the tone early in the century and in the novel:
face-to-face with Koljaiczek-Wranka, he makes no move to
unmask him, fearing for his own skin. Only when he is
'comfortably settled in the train' to Danzig does his right-
eousness begin to blossom, and even then he is careful not to
compromise himself: 'He did not actually denounce
Koljaiczek-Wranka; he merely entered a request that the
police look into the case, which the police promised to do.'
(p. 29). The SA volunteer Meyn is equally concerned about
his public image, frightened by disopprobium into sobriety:
'. . . he dreaded the neighbours in whose presence and
hearing he had sworn on numerous occasions that never
again would a drop of gin cross his musician's lips . . .'
(p. 193), attempting to cover the traces of his massacred cats
by dumping them in the dustbin. He is watched from another
apartment house window, denounced and expelled from the
SA for inhumanity to cats. The little enclosed world of the
apartment house, with its neighbourly nosiness and gossip,
acts as a court against petty transgressions and moulds the
conformity of its inmates.

The most significant example of discreet hypocrisy in the
novel is Agnes's affair with Jan Bronski. Their respective
degree of courage is well illustrated by their ways of playing
skat: 'Mama proposed at the very start that the stakes be
raised to a quarter of a pfennig, but this struck Uncle Jan as
took risky . . .' (p. 65). But Agnes's 'darling' is the product of
the fantasy life of a Madame Bovary rather than an active
disregard of public convention: she enjoys 'the delicious
misery of an adulterous woman's life' (p. 130), and acts out a
tragicomic version of romantic stereotypes, modelled on
Romeo and Juliet or 'the prince and the princess who
allegedly were unable to get together because the water was
too deep.' (p. 156). Her everyday behaviour is markedly
conformist: she is ashamed to have to parade Oskar in front
of other mothers on the first day of school (p. 73), and her

dieting schedules are ruined by secret orgies of eating
(p. 145). Attempting that cardinal sin against Nazi eugenics, to
abort Jan Bronski's child, she achieves only the appropriate
Liebestod of a *petit-bourgeois* Wagnerian – death through
over-eating. Her trips to the confessional and her guilt-laden
self-extinction demonstrate her fundamental adherence to the
Nazi stereotype of the chaste feminine ideal; in the Nazi
cinema 'all dishonoured women had to expiate their own
defilement through death.'[19] Torn between the German Matzerath and the Polish Bronski, Agnes illustrates the Cassubian
dilemma: 'we're not real Poles and we're not real Germans',
Oskar's grandmother tells him (p. 409); the political omens
draw her to Matzerath, her affection to Jan Bronski, and
she declines the responsibility of exercising choice.

The skat table is of course the central image of evasion in
the novel. Underneath, it provides perfect security for
discreet orgies, visible only to Oskar (who doesn't count, for
adults), Jan's sock offering 'woollen provocation' (p. 65) to
Agnes's genitals in debased parody of the heroics beneath the
grandmother's skirt, in Chapter One. Above, the childish adults
are at their play, the triangle providing a perfect formal
symmetry, the rules of the game a set of conventions which
relieve the individual of the agony of responsibility: '. . . in a
skat game at least you knew what to expect.' (p. 282). The
real world, with its complexity, irregularity and unpredict-
ability, is ritually banished: 'skat . . . was their refuge, their
haven, to which they always retreated when life threatened'
(p. 53).

Their behaviour thus exemplifies a monstrous imbalance
between the attention paid to trivia (the 'everyday world')
and the virtual abnegation of civic and political responsibility
(the 'historical'). The easy-going Matzerath is incensed only
by matters like his wife's smoking in public, which she does
on the way back from the Good Friday seaside outing (p. 148)
to provoke him (compare Nazi campaigns for women's
decency in public: '. . . the inhabitants of Erfurt were told by

their chief of police to stop women who smoked in public and remind them of their duties as German women and mothers')[20]. At the dinner celebrating Kurt's baptism, anger is aroused not by the indifference of the guests to the suffering of war but by Vincent Bronski's clumsiness:

> Ehlers, a native of the Baltic, showed a special aptitude for counting Russian prisoners; at every hundred thousand, a finger shot up; when his two outstretched hands had completed a million, he went right on counting by decapitating one finger after another. . . . Trying to impersonate a diving submarine, Vincent Bronski's left hand upset his beer glass. My grandmother started to scold him (p. 297).

And of course Meyn's expulsion from the SA offers fierce satiric comment on the schizophrenic morality of a society that glorifies his barbaric exploits during the *Kristallnacht* and is abhorred only by his inhumanity to cats!

Yet it should not be supposed that the novel's critical energies are directed only against the *petit-bourgeois*, and their habits. The rhetorical strategies are designed to implicate all of Oskar's post-war affluent readership; the audience, living 'a muddled kind of life outside this institution' (p. 13), sweating with '*Angst und Schrecken*' (Fear and Terror) in the Paris metro, contains liberal intellectuals as well as *petits bourgeois*. The flight from reality into theory receives the same scornful dismissal as the retreat to the skat table.

Thus the novel is full of idealistic theoreticians whose active and practical role in the real world is minimal. Oskar's visitors and friends, Klepp and Vittlar, are the first examples of the type, Klepp with his theories about the relation between jazz and Marxism (p. 34) or his elaborate schemes for organizing his life between sleep and propaganda (pp. 68-9), and Vittlar with his pseudo-philosophical jargon (pp. 34-5). Dr Hornstetter, Oskar's psychiatrist, theorizes about Oskar's inadequate contact with humanity, but seems to be in greater need of contact with him than he with her (p. 91). Dr Hollatz publishes long-winded irrelevancies on Oskar's glass-shattering powers (p. 67), to be emulated in due course by the pseudo-scientific explanations of the newspaper accounts of the damage at the Stadt-theater (p. 101). Amongst the Dusters, there is a clear split between the grammar-school theorists and the working-class activists: the Duster party doctrine is schoolboy anarchy '. . . our fight is against our parents and all other grown-ups, regardless of what they may be for or against.' (p. 367), and their activities take in such things as stealing church decorations and staging black masses – expressing their essentially conformist psychology in the frisson of wickedness and sacrilege these exploits provide them with. Their leader is the son of the Danzig police-chief. Meanwhile the only meaningful resistance activities are committed by the communist apprentices at the Schichau dockyards.

The essential thrust of Grass's analysis of the failures of German 'civil courage' during the Nazi period and after is that bourgeois respectability offers no kind of challenge to criminality. The emotional need to conform, the deep fear of individual action that might incur public condemnation, adapts itself equally strongly to malign and criminal publicly sanctioned attitudes as to harmless or benign ones. *Eichmann in Jerusalem*, Hannah Arendt's demythologizing study of Eichmann's trial in Israel, makes a similar point; for her, the man who organized the transportation of Jews to their execution was no demon but a petty conformist, throwing himself into the bureaucracy of genocide with the same energy as he gave to selling oil. She condemns him as well, but not for the crime for which he is convicted; she shows Nazi evil as banal rather than satanic. Oskar's view of criminals also denies them heroic status: 'In the very midst of their felonious pursuits the most desperate thieves, murderers, and incendiaries are just waiting for an opportunity to take up a more respectable trade.' (p. 24).

The hero of *The Tin Drum*, Oskar Matzerath, is fundamentally conceived as a subtle counter-image to these *petit-
bourgeois* evasions. The subtlety of the conception resides in
the fact that Oskar is by no means heroically opposed to the
skat-players of the novel; on the contrary, he practises the
same evasions, only in a systematic, conscious and above all
deliberate fashion. Oskar differs from his milieu only in that
he accepts responsibility, not for his role in private or
political events, but for his acts of evasion. In doing this he
offers a disturbing challenge to stereotyped notions of
'innocence.'

Oskar is essentially an ambiguous figure. The dwarf who
deliberately refuses to grow up, who decides to remain a
child and to evade adult responsibilities, blurs the conventional categories of 'child' and 'grown-up'; childishly
'innocent' in appearance, treated as such by adults, who drop
their pretenses in his presence, he is, nonetheless, fully
conscious, the reverse of 'childish' in his mental operations
and calculations. Similar conceptions abound in grotesque
art: the dwarf Miss Mowcher in *David Copperfield*, for
instance, speaks with an acute sophistication incongruous
with her childish appearance. Sexually neutral, she is allowed
access to intimate recesses of her customer's private lives, and
articulates a sharp consciousness of the gap between hypo-
critical pretensions and reality. Oskar is likewise a strate-
gically-placed instrument for uncovering the bad faith of
petit-bourgeois 'innocence'.

Oskar distances himself from grown-up childishness – as it
manifests itself for instance in a superstitious awe of material
objects '. . . there is something very strange and childish in
the way grown-ups feel about their clocks – in that respect, I
was never a child.' (pp. 62–3). He is sarcastic about the
concept of innocence: '. . . innocence is comparable to a
luxuriant weed – just think of all the innocent grandmothers
who were once loathsome, spiteful infants – no, it was not any
absurd reflections about innocence and lost innocence, that

made Oskar jump up from the kitchen chair . . .' (p. 491). Manheim's translation loses some of the bite and point of this passage: 'the little game of guilt and innocence' (*das Spielchen Schuld-Unschuld*) refers to the *faux naif* trivialization of issues of private and public responsibility practised so pervasively in the novel (cf. the shop-girl who blushes when Bruno asks for 'innocent' (*unschuldig*) white paper at the novel's opening). In sharp contrast to the childish adults of the novel, Oskar assumes total responsibility for his acts from the moment of birth; their retreat into irresponsibility is parodied by his sustained dissembling of childishness.

Thus Oskar's *deliberate* indifference to human suffering counterpoints the thoughtless negligence of his elders. In the chapter 'Good Friday Fare', for instance, Matzerath and Oskar are played off against each other: neither of them are at all moved to sympathy by Agnes's evident physical distress at the sight of the eel-catching. In Matzerath this is boyish self-absorption: he is excited and curious about the longshoreman's activities, he wants to help, he boasts about his haggling prowess, etc. By contrast, Oskar's attitude is a *calculated* detachment: his eyes remain fixed on the horizon, wondering whether the boat he sees is Finnish or Swedish, he notes details of the longshoreman's appearance with evident detachment, he even turns his account of Mama's vomiting into a callous joke: 'Even now Mama couldn't have vomited up more than half a pound and retch as she might, that was all the weight she succeeded in taking off.' (p. 145). He becomes tired of the arguments between the adults, and so calculates a means of distracting them: 'I drummed all the way to Brösen so they wouldn't start on again about eels.' (p. 148). Oskar's function here is to draw out the consequences implicit in 'normal' forms of bourgeois behaviour, to demonstrate their essential connections with his own aesthetic callousness. A similar point is made in the counterpointing of Oskar and Jan Bronski during the fall of the Polish post office: Bronski's retreat into the security of the skat-game expresses simple, compulsive cowardice, Oskar's parallel evasions are sarcastic and deliberate. The only 'risk' Oskar is willing to incur is that of playing skat for the first time in his life (thereby dropping his pretense of childishness, albeit ironically), the only 'responsibility' he takes on is that of distracting Bronski's fears: '...it would not have been hard for him to slip away between two of the shell hits which were shaking the building in quick succession, if a feeling of responsibility, such as he had never before experienced, had not bidden him hold on and counter his presumptive father's terror by the one effective means: skat-playing.' (p. 234). The ordeal at an end, Oskar resumes his normal 'irresponsible' role: 'I was separated from the thirty defenders by the wall. At this point Oskar remembered his gnomelike stature, he remembered that a three-year-old is not responsible for his comings and goings.' (p. 239). By a deliberate fiction, Oskar exposes the rationalizing fictions of 'innocence' practised by his fellow Germans.

In contrast to almost every character in the novel, Oskar *chooses* his social roles according to expediency: he is no Uncle Toby with a single hobbyhorse, but a virtuoso exponent of multiple, complex personae. To the Dusters he is Jesus Christ (the role providing them with the *frisson* of sacrilege that their bourgeois conception of rebelliousness seeks), but he drops this persona as soon as the game is up: 'I offered no resistance, but stepped automatically into the role of a snivelling three-year-old who had been led astray by gangsters.' (p. 374). For Sister Dorothea, Oskar adopts the role of Satan (p. 506), adapting himself to the needs of her repressions, which require sexual indulgence to be a diabolical rape, not (the theme of responsibility emerges once more) the consequences of her own desires. As a pop-star, Oskar manipulates his childhood again, using the nostalgia for the past that grows in the post-war years as a means of dispensing a comforting communal 'innocence' to his audiences: '. . . I succeeded in turning hardened old sinners into little children, singing Christmas carols in touching watery voices. 'Jesus, for thee I live, Jesus, for thee I die,' sang two thousand five hundred aged souls, whom no one would have suspected of such childlike innocence or religious zeal.' (p. 548). The same voices had been living and dying for some other leader a few years previously; Oskar's exploitation of their desire to be relieved of guilt is a cynically deliberate version of the same evasions.

Oskar's pleasure in complex role-playing is matched by his aesthetic tastes, which show a marked predilection for deviousness: 'May our Father in Heaven . . . discourage Oskar's penchant for the tortuous and labyrinthine.' (p. 45). He approves of Greff's complex and fantastical suicide-machine, which reminds him of Bruno's 'knotted string spooks' (p. 30). The operative word to describe Bruno's art is '*vielschichtig*' (elaborate or many-layered) and Oskar also uses it to characterize his notion of the fundamental aspects of human nature: '*menschlich* . . . *das heisst, kindlich, neugierig, vielschichtig, unmoralisch*' (human, that is, child-like, curious, complex and immoral) – (p. 75). Oskar likes to play games with words that imply ambiguity or multiplicity: 'Paradoxical: that might be the word for my feelings between Passion Monday and Good Friday.' (p. 141). The dwarf whose scenarios for the preservation of his detachment from life are complex works of art (the fall down the cellar, for instance – 'Not suicide, certainly not. That would have been too simple.' p. 58) – is an image of artistic irresponsibility, 'Oskar, the incorrigible aesthete' (p. 484).

The artist, the perpetrator of deliberate fictions, is a suspect figure in Grass's work. The conception of the artist as a liar, a purveyor of irresponsible imaginative games (which owes something to Thomas Mann), is frequent in Grass's mind, most evidently perhaps in some of his earlier political writings, where he is very self-conscious about his need to justify the artist's capability of engaging in 'real' life: 'Citizens of Lübeck . . . Someone is appearing before you whose profession is a suspect one: he writes fictional and yet suspiciously true-to-life stories.' (*Über das Selbstverständliche* p. 58). *The Tin Drum* displays many traces of a feeling of the fundamental bad faith of the artist, falsifying experience to create formally satisfying patterns, exploiting his past for money and fame – and most deviously of all – affecting a morality that may have its validity only in the idealizing world of fiction, that may not stand the test of practical application in everyday life. Hence Grass's powerful urge to make effective political contributions to German society; hence also, staying with the novel, some of Oskar's self-directed ironies about his aesthetic proclivities, on his decision to drum up the past, for instance: 'The time had come to transmute the pre-war and wartime experience of Oskar, the three-year-old drummer, into the pure, resounding gold of the post-war period.' (p. 542).

The critical energy and acuteness of *The Tin Drum* stems from this sceptical awareness of the artist's role. However 'pure' the intentions, however systematic the execution, the work of art for Grass can never stand outside the society that produces and consumes it. Even Oskar, the self-proclaimed hero, the systematic enemy of the *petit bourgeois*, the miraculously omniscient critic and manipulator of social convention, reflects fundamentally the tensions and contradictions of the society from which he springs. The obverse side of Oskar's cynical detachment is reflected in the evidently non-ironic longing for the security of the grandmother's skirts. Despite the images of labyrinths and tortuous corridors, Oskar's evident preference is for simple enclosed spaces that take a direct route back to the Cassubian potato field – the base of the Eiffel Tower for instance: '. . . the great vault, which seems so solidly closed despite spaces on all sides, became for me the sheltering vault of my grandmother Anna . . .' (p. 324). The house, as an image of security and permanence, has a powerful meaning for Oskar, and he is bitterly conscious that the constructions of architecture

are treacherous and do not provide the security under the
skirts: '. . . the Home Guards and I . . . stood amid
brick walls, in stone corridors, beneath ceilings with plaster
cornices, all so intricately interlocked with walls and parti-
tions that the worst was to be feared for the day when, in
response to one set of circumstances or another, all this
patchwork we call architecture would lose its cohesion.' (p.
241). The same applies for Danzig, the known extended space
now lost (Oskar's drum searches the Danzig shipyards for 'all
the hiding places that were ever known to me in those parts'
(p. 33)); the tone with which Oskar evokes its past is also
not ironic, contradicting the systematically affected cynical
pose: 'How I relished those afternoons in the multi-coloured
old city; there was always something of the museum about it
and there was always a peeling of bells from one church to
another.' (p. 95). And Oskar is a collector of momentoes of
the past, of photographs, documents, and drums – like Jan
Bronski of stamps or Klepp of portraits of the Royal Family.
The collector's passion, the minute attention to detail that
characterizes Oskar's realist art of narration, stems from the
source it despises – the grocer's shop with its routine of stock-
taking inventory. Grass has the visual and mental habit of
realist artists – James Joyce, who had an equal passion for
detail, once declared to Budgen, 'I have a grocer's assistant's
mind.'[21]

So the mind that unmercifully lashes the sins of the *petite
bourgeoisie* in *The Tin Drum* is itself fundamentally bourgeois.
The language of the novel allows this contradiction to develop
freely, for it carries the essential problematics contained in
The Tin Drum. In what way can the artist challenge stereotyped
perception, stimulate critical awareness, achieve any sort of
progressive function? The methods employed in *The Tin
Drum* are of a negative kind: Oskar's narrative can only imply
values that it cannot express. Fictions can only be dispelled,
in the world of this novel, through the adoption and recognition of deliberate fictions; humane forms of conduct can be

suggested only through the deliberate comic distortions of the grotesque.

NOTES

1. The first place I have found where Grass mentions the interconnectedness of the three novels is in an interview with Heinrich Vormweg, reprinted in Loschütz, p. 204.

2. Here I certainly do not intend criticism of John Reddick's *The 'Danzig Trilogy of Günter Grass'* (Secker & Warburg, 1975), which is the major study of the unity of the three novels. Reddick himself dismisses the idea of an overall formal unity in 'Eine epische Trilogie des Leidens? *Die Blechtrommel, Katz und Maus, Hundejahre*', *Text und Kritik* 1/1a (October 1971), pp. 39–40, arguing that the relationship between the parts is principally thematic and stylistic.

3. Laurence Sterne, *The Life and Opinions of Tristram Shandy* (Harmondsworth: Penguin Books, 1967), p. 192.

4. The quotations in this paragraph are taken from Kurt Lothar Tank, tr. John Conway, *Günter Grass* (New York: Frederick Ungar Publishing Co., 1969), pp. 70–71.

5. *Tristram Shandy*, ed. cit., p. 36.

6. Theodor Wieser makes the interesting point in his book that Grass's interest in the grotesque stems from his training in the visual arts (Wieser, pp. 34–5). Grass's drawings betray the clear influence of grotesque artists like Alfred Kubin.

7. Arnold, 'Gespräch mit Günter Grass', *Text und Kritik* 1/1a (October 1971), 5.

8. Lorenz, pp. 124–5.

9. This, and the following remarks are partially indebted to Thomas Cramer, *Das Groteske bei E. T. A. Hoffman* (Munich, 1966), pp. 20ff. and Wolfgang Kayser, *The Grotesque in Art and Literature* (New York: McGraw-Hill Book Company, 1966) passim.

10. Charles Dickens, *Our Mutual Friend* (London: Oxford University Press, 1952), pp. 79, 81.

11. Mikhail Bakhtin, *Rabelais and his World*, tr. Helene Iswolsky (Cambridge, Mass.: The M.I.T. Press, 1968), p. 49.

12. The passage is from the *Flüchtlingsgespräche, Gesammelte Werke* XIV, p. 1442.
13. This is a very simplified application of techniques of analysis practised by Wolfgang Iser in *The Implied Reader* (Baltimore, Md.: Johns Hopkins University Press, 1974).
14. Kosik, *Dialektik des Konkreten*, quoted in Georg Just, p. 53.
15. See Kayser, p. 68.
16. Reddick makes this point in *Text und Kritik* 1/1a, 39.
17. Just, p. 23.
18. Grunberger, p. 446.
19. ibid., p. 481.
20. ibid., p. 334.
21. Quoted in Richard Ellmann, *James Joyce* (New York: Oxford University Press, 1965), p. 28.

THE DANZIG TRILOGY II
Cat and Mouse

What I intend to describe
Can only refer to the button
That lay behind at Dunkirk,
Never the buttonless soldier that left.

Gesammelte Gedichte (*Collected Poems*):
'Abgelagert' (In Storage), p. 127.

After the publication of *The Tin Drum* in 1959, Grass quickly set to work on a new novel, which, as he declared to a Swiss visitor in the early part of 1960, 'takes for its theme the clichés of fascism, communism, and democracy – in other words a political novel, but a novel and not politics'.[1] At the annual meeting of the 'Gruppe 47' in Aschaffenburg in November 1960, Grass read a chapter from the new work, provisionally entitled *Kartoffelschalen* (Potato Peelings);[2] it was to end up, its original conception quite considerably revised, as the novel *Dog Years*. Grass obviously encountered difficulties in the execution of the work: 'Up until page 350 it was going all right, but then I seemed to run out of wind, and the method of narration started to become overstrained and artificial. The story *Cat and Mouse*, which was originally a part of the new novel, isolated itself from the rest of its own accord. After having broken down the original conception I was able to attack the plot of *Dog Years* afresh.'[3]

Cat and Mouse contains very clear traces of this origin,

with its constant reference to the material which produced
Dog Years, and *The Tin Drum*; its narrator Pilenz strives with
difficulty to avoid digression, to achieve concentrated focus
on the history of Mahlke, and refers with rueful irony to
stories like that of Brunies and Jenny which must be post-
poned until *Dog Years*: '. . . a dismal complicated story,
which deserves to be written, but somewhere else, not by me,
and certainly not in connexion with Mahlke.' (*Cat and Mouse*,
p. 38). The theme of the inexhaustibility of the Danzig
material is recognizable – Oskar Matzerath himself had
continually apologized for omissions and invoked divine aid
against digressions. Despite its relative concentration of form
(*Cat and Mouse* reads like a classical German *Novelle*, with
its emphasis on a single unifying incident, and there is evidence
that Grass studied this form carefully during the composition
of the work[5]) this volume of the trilogy contains the essential
idea that no single perspective can do justice to a plural
reality.

Cat and Mouse encountered controversy at an early stage of its
career. In the autumn of 1962 a petition from the Hesse Min-
istry of Labour, Health and Welfare was sent to Bonn, asking
that the book be placed on a list of writings that endanger
youthful morality; it cited various supposedly obscene
passages in the *Novelle* as evidence. A posse of eminent
champions of the work rose to its defence, and the petition
was withdrawn. Yet the incident may have helped to distort
the book's reception; what is most noticeable is the development of a kind of neo-Freudian orthodoxy, whereby the work
is a study of schizoid maladjustment (in the figure of Joachim
Mahlke) from social norms. This interpretation, proposed in
particular by a respected psychiatrist, Emil Ottinger,[5] has
tended to give the work a kind of protective normative
respectability.

Such a reading fits ill with the thematic unity of the Danzig
trilogy. *The Tin Drum* and *Dog Years* are patently anti-
Freudian works; we have already seen Oskar mock seekers of

THE DANZIG TRILOGY II

womb-imagery. Moreover, Ottinger's approach adopts a hermeneutics essentially foreign to Grass's work; it assumes a clear and unambiguous relation between surface and hidden meaning. The task for him is to decipher this relationship according to a body of knowledge external to the *Novelle* and given the status of proven truth. It is an assumption that runs through a great deal of criticism of Grass, and it of course enables a considerable number of rival interpretations, for the surface material is extremely rich and capable of being combined in a number of ways. I shall argue in this chapter that in this *Novelle*, and in Grass's work as a whole, surface is no more (and no less) than surface.

The psychological implications of *Cat and Mouse* (such as they are, for Grass as a writer seems in general far more preoccupied with sociology than with psychology) are primarily behaviouristic rather than psychoanalytic. The emphasis in Pilenz's account of Mahlke is on external and visible behaviour; Mahlke's 'unconscious', that hypothetical and certainly non-visible entity, remains inaccessible, to Pilenz at any rate. The narrator has to construct motives for Mahlke's conduct; Mahlke himself remains largely non-communicative about the contents of his soul, and the restriction of focus to the viewpoint of a single narrator of limited understanding (Pilenz is manifestly devoid of Oskar's omniscience) means that we have no other, or more authoritative viewpoint against which to check Pilenz's assumptions. There may be a 'ghost in the machine' that makes Mahlke tick, but it is essential to the story's strategy that this remain ambiguous and uncertain. Above all perhaps, it is essential for the reader to realize that what we are given is not a portrait of Mahlke as he is or was but of Pilenz's perception of him. It is hardly an exaggeration to say that the story is as much about Pilenz as about Mahlke; it certainly *reveals* more about the narrator than about the character he attempts, and essentially fails, to understand.

Pilenz is a conscientious narrator. In narrating the segment of his past that involves Mahlke, he seeks to provide an exacting factual accuracy, even on apparently insignificant matters. Unlike Oskar, he has no magical drum to provide him with total recall; rather more like Brauxel/Amsel, he avails himself on occasions of fetishistic *aide-memoires*, objects or substances designed to provide Proustian evocation of the past: 'Perhaps if I rubbed my typewriter superficially with onion juice, it might communicate an intimation of the onion smell which in those years contaminated all Germany, West Prussia and Langfuhr . . .' (*Cat and Mouse*, p. 93). Yet he is self-consciously aware of the irrationality of these methods, and more characteristically pursues the sober historian's method, carefully assessing and presenting evidence, cross-checking it, and searching for internal contradictions. To give an accurate description of Mahlke's facial appearance, he consults with other contemporaries, and presents an agreed composite (p. 35); relating Mahlke's exploits in the Reich Labour Service, he offers the statements of four observers, acceptable evidence because free of contradiction (p. 107). Whenever Pilenz is uncertain of his assertions, he expresses this openly: '. . . maybe the stickiness of my hands is only an idea that came to me later, maybe they were not sticky at all.' (p. 22). The impression of scrupulous honesty is heightened by the immediacy with which Pilenz corrects mis-statements; when he asserts that Mahlke's screwdriver wasn't noticed in church, he immediately retracts: 'No, there I'm going too far. It would certainly not have escaped me.' (p. 16; Pilenz is even sharper in German: '*Falsch! Mir wäre das Ding bestimmt nicht entgangen.*') 'Your house was in Westerzeile. . . . No, your house was on Osterzeile.' (p. 18).

What does Pilenz's thirst for accuracy signify? Its frequent deployment for trivia – Pilenz is careful to inform us that both the gramophone and the fire-extinguisher fished from the minesweeper are of German make (p. 21), and resembles Oskar Matzerath in his capacity to tell the number of engines in an airplane from its sound (p. 5) – suggests an ironic purpose. Pilenz is unaware of the fact that his taste for minutiae derives from ingrained schoolboy habits of compiling and reciting rather pointless facts: 'The Polish fleet was small but ambitious. We knew its modern ships, for the most part built in England or France, by heart, and could reel off their guns, tonnage and speed in knots with never a mistake, just as we could recite the names of all Italian light cruisers, or of all the obsolete Brazilian battleships and monitors.' (p. 27). And the *Novelle* pointedly conveys how such habits, fostered by an educational system that combines militaristic nationalism with rote-learning, cocoon the schoolboys from the realities of war that lie behind statistics – suffering, death, irretrievable loss.

So Pilenz's mental equipment for uncovering the 'truth' about the past and his relation to Mahlke looks unpromising. The motive for his narration is a desire to unburden himself of the guilt he has accumulated concerning Mahlke: that he may have been responsible for goading the cat to attack Mahlke's Adam's Apple, that this may have caused Mahlke to compensate for his inadequacies, that he was a bystander and betrayer as Mahlke commits suicide. But the technique of documentary thoroughness offers no answers to these doubts. The story of the cat's attack on Mahlke's mouse is presented in several versions, none of them definitive; there is no conclusive evidence to show whether Mahlke died deliberately or accidentally, or whether indeed he died at all. *Cat and Mouse* is about skepsis, the essential irreducibility of experience and its unamenability to unambiguous proof.

Pilenz is a born agnostic. At school, he is non-committal, unable to make up his mind whether to volunteer for military service, and if so, which branch to enter: '. . . me who kept hesitating whether to go into the Navy or not . . .' (p. 77). The cat-and-mouse story torments him because he is unable to decide where his sympathies lie: 'If I saw a cat, whether grey or black or pepper-and-salt, the mouse ran into my field of vision forthwith; but still I hesitated, undecided whether the mouse should be protected or the cat goaded into catching it.' (p. 99). He is ironically conscious of his inability to commit himself: 'Hesitation was my trouble; I haven't got over it yet, and this weakness of mine still inspires me with the same ironical reflections.' (p. 99). And so the Pilenz who narrates the story of Mahlke is now secretary of a Catholic centre in Düsseldorf, still uncertain whether he believes in the dogma '. . . I was never sure and to this day I am not sure, whether there might not after all be something behind or in front of the altar or in the tabernacle . . .' (pp. 44–5), still searching for proofs and certainties: 'Over tea brewed much too black, I spend whole nights discussing the blood of Christ, the Trinity, and divine penance with the Franciscan Father Alban, who is an open-minded man though more or less a believer.' (p. 78).

Pilenz's inability to settle his account with the Catholic Church is a very exact parallel to his difficulties in understanding Mahlke. In both cases the problem is a question of relating external signs, images and emblems to their internal meaning, a question of what is 'behind' the surface level. He is entirely conscious of the problem: '. . . as for his soul, it was never introduced to me. I never heard what he thought. In the end, all I really had to go by was his neck and its numerous counterweights.' (p. 29). The men who relate Mahlke's exploits in the Labour Service camp acknowledge the same difficulty: 'Seems there was more to it than sex. You never know the whole story,' (p. 108, the translation not quite in focus; '*man guckt ja nie durch*' is literally 'you can never really see what's at the bottom of it.') Pilenz is a materialist, and he is searching for Mahlke's soul as if it might be something tangible or visible, to be seized through observation, as when Mahlke is praying: 'His joined hands dropped below his collarbone and his mouth smelled as though a pot of cabbage were simmering on a small flame within him.' (p. 89).

Cat and Mouse is by no means the only work of Grass in

THE DANZIG TRILOGY II   57

which the relationship between material objects and intangible essences has a part to play. Grass can be seen in relation to writers of the *nouveau roman* in France, especially to Robbe-Grillet, with his uncomprising behaviourist rejection of the human significance of objects; all that can be described for Robbe-Grillet is the surface of phenomena, any assumption of an unseen principle behind that surface is humanist sentimentality or 'bad faith[6]'. While Grass is likewise a consistent anti-idealist, there remains, probably as a result of his Cassubian, catholic background, a residue of superstitious animism; things, in Grass's work, are alive with magical properties as they are in the novels of Balzac or Dickens. The characteristic tone, in dealing with human projections of significance onto inanimate or incorporeal objects is teasing, skeptical, ironic. The question, rather as in Pilenz's dealings with catholicism, remains perpetually open as in 'Diana – or the Objects', where the goddess's arrow strikes the observer's soul as if it had a tangible reality:

> When she hit me
> her object hit my soul
> which is to her like an object.
>
> *Poems of Günter Grass* (p. 38)

In *The Tin Drum*, the photograph of Oskar's mother shows eyes 'which seem to look upon the souls of her fellow men – and her own soul as well – as solid objects, something like teacups or cigarette holders.' (p. 50). The satire of Agnes Matzerath's *petit bourgeois* materialism is obvious enough, but its perspective does not exclude the possibility that the soul may exist compounded of less prosaic material.

One other incident in *Cat and Mouse* illuminates the problem of the relation between matter and spiritual essence; in a grotesquely comic parallel to Pilenz's search for Mahlke's soul. Father Gusewski's hand goes groping down the back of Pilenz's shorts: 'Once when I was about thirteen, he ran his small, hairless hand down my back under my shirt from my neck to the waist of my gym shorts, but stopped there because my shorts had no elastic band and I tied them in front with tapes . . . all perfectly harmless, it was really my Catholic soul he was looking for.' (p. 87). Pilenz's irony is gentle; the priest's soul-seeking founders on one of those prosaic materialist details (the missing elastic band) that are likewise a barrier to reaching Mahlke's soul. The mind of the narrator is one that can 'see through' Gusewski (as it does with Dr Klohse and the Conradinium and the military heroes paraded at the school) but cannot bring itself to outright rejection. Pilenz is a finely poised conception: on the one hand sympathetically portrayed, not without dignity in his painstaking attempts to reconstruct and come to terms with the 'truth' of the past, on the other hand painfully limited, preoccupied with the accumulation of surface details that can achieve no resolution of his anguish, his skeptical irony a non-committal pose, expressing the desire to perpetuate the summers of lazing and musing on the mine-sweeper: 'Once again, before it is too late, let me turn over on my back and contemplate the great clouds shaped like potato sacks, which rose from Putziger Wiek and passed over our barge in endless procession, providing changes of light and cloud-long coolness.' (p. 77). Pilenz's cast of mind, and more than a few details of his biography – he too saw military service in Cottbus and lands after the war in Düsseldorf – suggest that he is a partial image of Grass himself; if so, he is an instrument for 'calling into question' the validity of the integrity of post-war skeptical intellectuals who start out to write like Kafka (cf. p. 96).

Turning to Mahlke's 'case', the need is first to challenge the orthodox neo-Freudian view that he is a latent 'schizoid' maladjusted to society. There is something rather disturbing, even shocking about the application of a normative psychology to a *Novelle* critical of Nazi society; as if it were not the 'maladjusted' members of that society, people like Anton Schmidt or the Scholls, who provide the only worthwhile 'norms', to the shame of the conformist pusillanimity of the

mass of Germans. Emil Ottinger is evidently happy to accept
Dr Klohse and Father Gusewski as representative of the
'decent' social norm (he describes Klohse as 'the representative of order, unyielding but moderate, not without decency',
and endorses Father Gusewski's anxieties about Mahlke)[7]; the
Novelle is as unambiguous as may be in exposing their
hypocrisy. The self-proclaimed objectivity of such a psychology asks to be questioned critically – as do those com-
mentators on the work who accept Ottinger as an authoritative reference. Even a more sophisticated interpretation like
Irène Leonard's (she accepts the sickness of the society
portrayed in *Cat and Mouse*, but sees Mahlke's protest only
as a useless one, lacking in political judgment)[8] unconsciously
reflects a standard rationalization, that protest in Nazi
Germany was 'practically useless' – drawing from Hannah
Arendt this retort: '. . . nothing can ever be "practically
useless," at least, not in the long run. It would be of great
practical usefulness for Germany today, not merely for her
prestige abroad but for her sadly confused inner condition, if
there were more such stories to be told.'[9]

This is not to suggest that 'the great Mahlke' is to be
regarded as a hero of legendary proportions, on a level with
Parsifal or Christ – an equally misleading temptation to
critics (not wholly eschewed by Cunliffe in his otherwise
valuable study of the work.[10]) If a fictional parallel to Mahlke
is needed, the most relevant to me seems Don Quixote – a
figure Grass uses quite frequently, in *The Tin Drum* or in the
poem 'Pan Kiehot' (*Gesammelte Gedichte*, p. 117), as an
image of madcap Polish bravery, idealism, foolery, melancholy. Mahlke has features in common with Don Quixote –
his physical angularity, his devotion to an idealized lady (the
Virgin Mary, the Queen of Poland – cf. Vincent Bronski in
The Tin Drum), his chaste and fastidious aloofness. He is
essentially a grotesque, ambivalent, tragicomic hero, acting
and reacting in a world complexly layered with illusions and
realities, not an idealized epic figure.

c

Like Oskar Matzerath, Mahlke possesses a grotesque physique, its proportions defying classical rules; where penis balances hump in the case of Oskar, with Mahlke the penis counterpoints his outsize Adam's apple: 'strangely enough, the length of the sexual part made up for the otherwise shocking protuberance of his Adam's apple, lending his body an odd, but in its way perfect harmony.' (*Cat and Mouse*, p. 33). Also like Oskar, though in more muted form, Mahlke has quasi-miraculous powers; his capacity to produce 'mighty streams' of semen in quick succession after each other, his extraordinary diving exploits, hover on the edges of the fantastic, teasing our perceptions of the 'normal' and the mythical. Most importantly, perhaps, Mahlke resembles Oskar in his dwarf-function; he too wants to be a clown, and gets his laughs through his deformities. But the laughter he provokes is uneasy and ambiguous:

> But when Dr Brunies . . . asked the boys of our class what profession they were planning to take and you . . . said: 'I'm going to be a clown and make people laugh,' no one laughed in the classroom – and I myself was frightened. For while Mahlke firmly and candidly stated his intention of becoming a clown in a circus or some-where else, he made so solemn a face that it was really to be feared that he would one day make people laugh themselves sick, if only by publicly praying to the Virgin between the lion tamer and the trapeze act; but that prayer of yours on the barge must have been in earnest – or wasn't it? (p. 19).

Pilenz's uncertainties about this ambiguous humorist poses the question: what does Mahlke's desire to become a clown mean? In the nature of the work there can be no clear answer, but his choice of a career may be a cryptic comment on the absurdity of asking the question of schoolboys in wartime; apart from becoming soldiers and being killed, few opportunities are open to these children (Oskar finds professional clowning the only means of evading being drafted or certified during wartime). Mahlke is distinguished by his taciturnity; he uses words with economy and precision (in sharp contrast both to the luxuriant slang of the schoolboys or the poetic, idealist *kitsch* uttered by Dr Klohse and the military heroes) whenever he breaks his characteristic silence, giving 'simple, modest explanations' (p. 41) when he comments on his exploits on the minesweeper, or quietly quoting 'chapter and verse from the Service regulations' when he is asked to build a rabbit-hutch by his commanding officer (p. 108; the key German word in both these passages is *sachlich*). Longer utterances are characteristically cryptic: 'Now they need a bag of forty if they want the medal. At the beginning and after they were through in France and in the North, it only took twenty – if it keeps on like this . . .' (p. 51). When Mahlke returns to the subject of his vocation as a clown, he places it above a military career: '. . . I'd rather do something useful or funny.' (p. 90).

To 'do something useful'; the tragic aspect of Mahlke's career is that war denies him any outlet for energy other than destruction and death. Grunberger's acute social history of Nazi Germany analyzes the condition of German youth in wartime:

> When the outbreak of war inaugurated a succession of lightning victories, many who were too young to participate in the fighting experienced feelings of acute frustration. At the height of the war neutral observers noticed that even children were affected by the general mood of tension and expectancy; expectancy in their case took the form of grandiose post-war dreams, in which they saw themselves as Gauleiters in such remote parts of the globe as Africa, India or South America, whilst others had their imagination fired by Himmler's project for dotting vast spaces of the Slavic East with the fortified farms of German overlords.[11]

Throughout *Cat and Mouse* Mahlke seems to yearn for activity, for means of absorbing his energies: 'Mahlke didn't make things easy for himself; while we dozed on the barge, he worked under water.' (p. 12). He can only find meaningless, repetitive things to do: feverish collecting for the *Winterhilfswerk*, fishing out treasures from the wreck and then putting them all back again: 'But what we admired most about this game of removal man, which went on for days, was precisely its absurdity and deliberate destructiveness.' (p. 58). This 'deliberate destructiveness' reflects the anarchic forces unleashed by a society engaged in aggressive war; Mahlke confirms Oskar's diagnosis of 'your incorrigible partisan, who undermines what he has just set up.' (*The Tin Drum*, p. 416), and it is no accident that Mahlke's nose for hideaways leads him to uncover a partisan depot. At the front, Mahlke takes to drawing pictures of tanks as a means of self-expression, but over this outlet for energy stands the sign of the bankruptcy of Nazi education: 'squiggly line drawings under neat Sütterlin script.' (*Cat and Mouse*, p. 101).

Nonetheless, the few moments of mature, humane consciousness that emerge from the world described in *Cat and Mouse* belong to Mahlke. He remains impervious to the militaristic propaganda dispensed in school and Hitler youth-camps: 'You know how I feel about all that stuff: militarism, playing soldier, the current overemphasis on martial virtues.' (p. 90). Gently and delicately he chides his adult aunt for her prurient interest in Pilenz's mother's sordid affairs with army officers: 'Never mind about that, Auntie. Who can afford to judge in times like this when everything is topsy-turvy.' (p. 94). Mahlke's 'soul' that so comprehensively evades Pilenz's attempt to locate it, an organ of moral perception inviolable to the pressures of social conformity, is glimpsed in these moments; and if Mahlke's end is indeed an act of 'deliberate self-destruction', then it may perhaps express a melancholy consciousness of 'topsy-turvy' times in which suicide is one of the few meaningful actions left open

(Mahlke is in the company of Walter Benjamin). Compared
with this perception, Klohse's notion of adulthood '*Reif-
werdenreinbleiben*', (Mature but pure) – is a travesty: Mahlke
is whatever norm *Cat and Mouse* has to offer.

'I have tried to explain, how boring and frightful war is on
a day-to-day basis, how little place there is for heroics.'[12]
Whilst Mahlke frantically seeks meaningful activity, and finds
none, the other children react to the same pressures by
becoming bored. Their activities on the wreck – chewing
slime, spotting ships entering the harbour – express a state of
inertia: 'We clasped our slightly trembling knees, chewed gull
droppings into a sludge; half weary, half fascinated we
counted a formation of Navy cutters . . .' (p. 13). The
masturbation olympics, complete with tape-measure, stop-
watch and a set of rules, are devised as a means of passing the
time: '. . . we decided to give our swimming trunks a rest and
sprawled naked on the rusty bridge, with very little idea what
to do with ourselves.' (p. 30). Boringly they are reminded by
the military visitors at the Conradinium that war-time can be
boring. Air Force Lieutenant: '. . . well, boys, don't get the
idea that life in the Air Force is like a rabbit hunt, all action
and never a dull moment. Sometimes nothing happens for
whole weeks.' (p. 47). Lieutenant Commander: '. . . you can
imagine, living on a sardine tin in the middle of the Atlantic
or the Arctic, cramped humid hot, men obliged to sleep on
spare torpedoes, nothing stirring for days on end, empty
horizon...' (p. 64) and their predictable reaction is to be bored.

Mahlke gains their approval because he is an antidote to
boredom. They seek to relieve their boredom through
sensations and curiosities; the operative word to describe
what they seek is '*doll*', *plattdeutsch* for 'fabulous' or 'terrific.'
When Pilenz's girl cousins arrive from Berlin, the hope is 'to
do something really wild (*etwas Dolles*) with them, we didn't
know what. (p. 39); when Zarah Leander is heard from the
underwater gramophone she produces the right sensation,
'*den dollsten Effekt.*' (p. 59). Mahlke's gift is to be able to

provide '*was Dolles*', whether it be a piece of treasure from the wreck ('something really special' (p. 6), a secret hideaway. Even the Third Formers had heard rumours of an amazing (*dollen*) and amazingly furnished hideaway inside the bridge' (p. 85), or a stolen medal ('Terrific *doll*)! Let me touch it.' – (p. 80). Mahlke is a 'fab guy' (*Doller Bursche*), both for the boys (p. 75 – 'What a chap!') and for his comrades in the Labour Service (he is regarded as having done some 'mighty sensational (*dolle*) things' – p. 107.) A summer without Mahlke on the minesweeper (p. 84) is a disaster.

'In my Novelle *Cat and Mouse* . . . I have undertaken the attempt at portraying the fabrication of a military hero by society . . .'13. The origins of that fabrication lie in the needs of schoolboys to construct idols – with appropriately outsize sexual equipment: 'Mahlke's was first of all a size thicker, second a match-box longer, and third looked much more grown-up, dangerous, and worthy to be worshipped.' (p. 32). He becomes a legend through Pilenz's application of a magic title, 'The Great Mahlke'; 'And the title stuck. All previous attempts to fasten nicknames to Mahlke had been shortlived.' (p. 75). As in *The Tin Drum*, adults vie with these adolescents in childishness; Brunies sucks sweets, the 'boyish' Father Gusewski plays pingpong in the sacristy with the altar boys (p. 87), and Mahlke's mother and aunt gape at the boy's grasp of military know-how: 'When he rattled off the names of the Italian *esploratori*, both women gaped in astonishment and Mahlke's aunt clapped her bony hands resoundingly; there was something girlish about her enthusiasm, and in the silence that followed her clapping, she fiddled with her hair in embarrassment.' (p. 95). The essential continuity between the glamour of 'dirty tricks' for the schoolchildren and the glamour of military heroics is conveyed in the language of children's games employed both by the Air Force Lieutenant and the Navy Commander: 'On the very first mission a formation with a fighter escort came straight at us, and believe me, it was a real merry-go-round' (p. 47); '. . . when

we bagged our first tanker, the *Arndale*, 17,200 tons, with two
fish amidships, believe it or not, I thought of you, my dear
Dr Stachnitz, and began to recite out loud, without turning
off the intercom, *qui quae quod, cuius cuius cuius* . . . until our
exec called back. Good work, skipper, you may take the rest
of the day off.' (p. 64); (the last sentence might better be
translated 'no school today.') In the Air Force Lieutenant's
speech the language of the swimming-pool makes the link
with the exploits on the sunken minesweeper quite unmistakeable: '*da routiert er im Bach, aber auch ich bin kurz
vorm Badengehen*' 'he drops into the pond, but I'm pretty near
taking a dip myself' (p. 47, Manheim's translation not quite
specific enough).

Mahlke seems to 'play along' with the role with which he is
presented. Despite Pilenz's insistence that Mahlke depends on
an audience, the evidence he produces to support this view is
inconsistent and contradictory: 'Applause did him good and
quietened the jumping mouse on his throat; applause also
embarrassed him and started the selfsame mouse up again.'
(p. 23). Compliments, interest and curiosity are met with
Mahlke staring into the distance or continuing his activity
undisturbed. He holds himself at a distance, keeping in
reserve an ambivalent consciousness of the nullity of the
glory he covets and attains, aware of the minimal outlets of
expression this society permits.

Pilenz, having played a significant role in the mythologizing
of Mahlke, setting himself up as the intermediary between
Mahlke and the admiring mob, is engaged in the narrative in
an attempted demythologizing. The thrust of the work's
meaning is that only by commitment, by effective and active
engagement, can the ghost of the past be laid.

NOTES

1. Quoted in Tank, p. 94.
2. See Reinhard Lettau, ed., *Die Gruppe 47 – Bericht Kritik*

Polemik (Neuwied and Berlin: Hermann Luchterhand Verlag, 1967), p. 157.
3. See Loschütz, p. 214.
4. According to Reddick in *The Danzig Trilogy of Günter Grass*, p. 89, quoting the testimony of Walter Höllerer.
5. 'Zur mehrdimensionalen Erklärung von Straftaten Jugendlicher am Beispiel der Novelle *Katz und Maus* von Günter Grass', *Monatsschrift für Kriminologie und Strafrechtsreform* (May/June, 1962), reproduced in Loschütz, pp. 38–48.
6. See Just, pp. 122–3, and also John Fletcher, *New Directions in Literature* (London: Calder & Boyars, 1968), pp. 150–3, for an exploration of the relation of the *nouveau roman* to behaviourist psychology.
7. Ottinger in Loschütz, p. 46.
8. Irène Leonard, *Günter Grass* (Edinburgh: Oliver & Boyd, 1974), pp. 26–36.
9. Hannah Arendt, *Eichmann in Jerusalem: A Report on the Banality of Evil* (New York: The Viking Press, 1965), p. 233.
10. Cunliffe, pp. 87–97.
11. Grunberger, p. 346.
12. *Text und Kritik* 1/1a, p. 49.
13. ibid., p. 49.

THE DANZIG TRILOGY III
Dog Years

'History offers us no comfort. It hands out hard lessons. It makes absurd reading, mostly. Admittedly it moves on, but progress is not the result of history. History is never-ending: we are always inside history, never outside it!

Günter Grass: Dokumente zur Politischen Wirkung
(p. 225)

Dog Years is Grass's most ambitious and difficult novel. It has the same three-part structure as *The Tin Drum* (early twentieth century, Nazi period, post-war period), but the patterns of the earlier novel are multiplied; instead of a single narrative perspective, there is a three-man 'author's collective', whose stories overlap and contradict each other, instead of a relatively simple time-scheme in which past and present are clearly differentiated and ordered (Oskar's narrative takes us chronologically from his origins to the point in the present where the novel begins), the narrative techniques of *Dog Years* intermingle past and present, jumping associatively forward and back so that (like *Ulysses*) it has to be read at least twice before its patterns become clear. In addition, there is a whole new dimension of time: the novel is not only about the relation of present to immediate past, but refers us back to the whole recorded history of the Danzig area, and beyond, to a mythic past.

67

This extra dimension highlights essential features of the work: *Dog Years* is a historical novel, taking as its subject the way in which the accumulations of the past (including its myths) help to shape and determine the present. Right at the beginning of the novel, the first narrator Brauxel invokes the river Vistula as an image of the course of history, a kind of preserving fluid in which concrete evidence of the reality of the past is gathered: 'What had long been forgotten rose to memory, floating on its back or stomach, with the help of the Vistula: Pomeranian princes. Adalbert came. Adalbert comes on foot and dies by the axe. But Duke Swantopolk allowed himself to be baptized. What will become of Mestwin's daughters? Is one of them running away barefoot? Who will carry her off? The giant Milligedo with his lead club? Or one of the ancient gods? The fiery-red Perkunos? The pale Pikollos, who is always looking up from below? The boy Potrimpos laughs and chews at his ear of wheat. Sacred oaks are felled. Grinding teeth – and Duke Kynstute's young daughter, who entered a convent . . .' (p. 11–12). And so on, through the age of Renaissance bandits, Frederick the Great, and the Napoleonic wars to the present. It is a history of violence and strife, from the martyrdom of St Adalbert (who came to convert the heathen Prussians), through the militant crusading history of the Teutonic Knights who drove the heathens into the forests of Lithuania in order to create a Germanic 'christian' state, through the religious and sectarian struggles and persecutions, Catholic against Protestant or Hussite or Mennonite, Christian against Jew, down to the age of genocide. Its course is irregular and tangled; now one side holds ascendancy, now another; periods of war alternate with periods of peace, as one group fights fiercely for survival, another submits; Adalbert is murdered by Prussian heathens but Swantopolk chooses to be converted, Kynstute resists the Teutonic crusaders but his daughter enters a convent. Its effects upon the present are real and tangible: Mennonites continue to burn down Catholic mills; Amsel inherits and experiences the antisemitism of a poor, superstitious agrarian community; Walter Matern is influenced by the anarchic violence of Renaissance ancestors, and by the expedient tergiversations of their successors; Tulla Pokriefke bears the Christian name of Kynstute's daughter. The narrative leaps associatively from the Prussian fertility god Potrimpos, chewing wheat, to the gnashing teeth of Walter Matern.

The subject demands breadth and depth for its exposition. In *Dog Years*, everyone and everything, down to the most apparently trivial detail, has a history, and bears its marks; the epic dimensions staked out in the image of the Vistula and its debris, the passion for detail evinced by Brauxel and compelled on his co-authors, require that these histories be narrated. The Pokriefkes are from Koshnavia, and the tangled history of that territory, first under the heathen Pomeranian dukes, then under Teutonic Knights, Polish and Prussian kings, up until the Polish republic of the interwar years and then Hitler's conquest and defeat, must be rehearsed: 'Violence. Bent safety pins. Pennants in the wind. Billeting. Swedes Hussites Waffen-SS. Andifyoudon't. Rootandbranch. Asoffourfortyfivethismorning. Circles described with compasses on military maps. Schlangenthin taken in counterattack. Anti-tank spearheads on the road to Damerau ... In line with the decision to straighten the front, the so-called territory of Koshnavia is evacuated.' (p. 140). Centuries of past voices are mingled; the aggressive demands of 1939 merge imperceptibly with the euphemistic evasions of 1944. Successive invaders leave traces, flags and bent safety-pins: the deposit of history.

Stutthof, the site of the Nazi's first Polish concentration camp, has a history too, that needs relating for readers who may have somehow forgotten it. Rats have a history: 'The same old song since the days of Noah. Rat stories, true and made-up. ... Egypt's lean years. And when Paris was besieged. And when the rat sat in the tabernacle. ... And when they carried the plague back and forth and pierced the pink flesh of pigs. When they devoured the Bible and multiplied in accordance with its instructions. When they disemboweled the clocks and confuted time. When they were sanctified in Hamelin.' (p. 328). Ballet has a history, and Felsner-Imbs is its representative: 'No-one doubted that this was an eyewitness to historical performances: thus he must have been present when, in the early romantic days of the last century, la Taglioni, la Grisi, Fanny Cerito and Lucile Grahn danced the famous *Grand Pas de Quatre* and were showered with roses.' (p. 190). The Oliva zoo has a history, and its proprietor loves to recount it (p. 219); even trees in the forest have a history: 'In the rain outside the windows stood pine trees full of squirrels and the Prussian past.' (p. 316). SA men have a history too, and during the thirties they delight in recounting beer-hall stories of brawls of the past – 'And one time at the Café Derra! You're nuts, man, that was in Zinglers Höhe, they beat Brill up. And then another time, only a couple of days ago. Where was that?' (p. 212); after the war, their memories become more reticent. The force that impels Brauxel and his team of narrators is the desire to preserve the past from post-war lapses of the German memory; Matern, with his avenging forays from the Cologne station men's lavatory, and Brauxel, with his dredging of the Vistula to ensure that the lost pen-knife be found, attempt to uncover historical origins and causes, to rescue buried or conveniently forgotten realities from oblivion. 'History . . . has an elephantine memory.' (*Günter Grass: Dokumente zur politischen Wirkung* – p. 219).

In an important essay, 'On my teacher Döblin,' Grass describes the work of the writer whom he regards as the most important influence on his own work, and gives plentiful insights into his own conception of the historical novel. Grass claims for Alfred Döblin – little known outside Germany, except as the author of *Berlin Alexanderplatz*, a novel that applies the technique of *Ulysses* to the depiction of the struggle and failures of a criminal released from jail, attempting to survive in the Berlin of the twenties – the status of a modern classic, to stand beside Brecht and Thomas Mann; he singles out for praise Döblin's historical novel *Wallenstein*. It is Döblin the realist, the anti-idealist recorder of the complexities and contradictions of history that Grass admires: 'Döblin sees history as an absurd process. No Hegelian *Weltgeist* rides over the battlefields for him.' Döblin's Wallenstein is a financier – the Alfred Krupp of the Thirty Years War – pursuing war as a means of furthering his commercial aims, not a heroic military commander acting from idealistic notions of honour and glory; his actions cannot be understood as an expression of a historical logic: 'Schiller was concerned to portray the Thirty Years War as an articulated, apprehendable whole. One thing stems from another. His hand makes order, binds relationships together, wants to make sense of things. Consciously and continuously Döblin shatters all that to pieces, so that reality can emerge.' Grass praises Döblin's futurist techniques of destroying the concept of historical logic through the simultaneous juxtaposition of apparent irrelevancies, describing him as 'the cool, as if impartial observer of forces in motion and reality with its contradictions, the registrar of simultaneous movements, acting as a brake and extinguisher on each other.'[1]

It is quite evident that *Dog Years* shares this conception of history as an 'absurd process', and utilizes similar techniques to reveal it as such. George Steiner notes the employment of somewhat 'old-fashioned' narrative devices in *Dog Years* (though he, writing before the publication of the Döblin essay, ascribes their origin to Dos Passos);[2] they express of course Grass's adherence to the 'heroic' early phase of modernism blotted out in the Nazi period. The central device of the dogs and their history, played simultaneously against the more momentous background of the rise and impact of the Nazi party, is a sometimes crude but powerful means of focussing the 'absurd' connections between private and public history.

The dogs of *Dog Years* (like everything else) have their history, a pedigree stretching back to remote semi-mythical origins in Lithuania, the last refuge of the heathen Prussians: 'In the obscure beginnings there is said to have been, there was, in Lithuania a she-wolf, whose grandson, the black dog Perkun, sired the bitch Senta; and Pluto covered Senta; and Senta whelped six puppies, among them the male Harras; and Harras sired Prinz; and Prinz will make history in books that Brauxel does not have to write.' (p. 66). The joke is clear: the dogs parody the mythical Aryan origins claimed for the Germans by Hitler and his racist pseudo-authorities, the stock represented at its purist in the Teutonic races themselves (*'Bin echt deutsch, stamm' aus Litauen'*). They are given the names of gods and heroes (Perkun=Prussian thundergod); they are racially 'pure', as black as an SS uniform on a black-bird (*'amselschwarz'*, ironically like the 'impure' Eddi Amsel – see p. 139). The promiscuity of language in the novel allows dogs and humans to become easily muddled; when Harry Liebenau goes to the police station to accompany Harras on his eugenic exploits he sees twenty-five photographs pinned up – twenty-four of police dogs, one of Hindenburg, looking very much like a bloodhound, 'an elderly man in a spiked helmet, with tired eyes under heavy eyelids.' (p. 154). Harry's father is so proud that his dog has been chosen for stud purposes that 'an onlooker could easily have been led to believe that the police had called not upon Harras but upon my father to mate.' (p. 152); the Liebenaus look upon themselves as connected with the Materns via their dogs, so that Walter Matern might have been regarded as our relation, because his father's shepherd bitch Senta had whelped our Harras.' (p. 176). Harras's kennel is his 'Reich' – like the thousand-year version, rather impermanent, for Liebenau hacks it down when the war starts to go wrong. When Harry and Jenny visit the cinema, keenly scanning the newsreel for a glimpse of Hitler with Prinz at his side, they see only rather inferior dogs: 'We were both disappointed when only Keitel,

Jodl and somebody else were standing around him amid trees on gravel paths.' (p. 308). Hardly surprisingly, then, Walter Matern in his drunkenness torments Harras by yelling the word 'Nazi!' into his kennel. (p. 264). But the absurdity of history in *Dog Years* is realized not only in these playful metaphoric correspondences but in the actual contour of events. Significant happenings stem from trivial causes; momentous upheavals seem to produce very little change; apparently opposite historical forces appear in incongruous juxtaposition. At all levels, the absurd trivia of everyday life intertwine with the great forces of history, reflecting each other in parallel, repetition or parody. Liebenau joins the Nazi party as the result of the fame of his dog Harras. Senta reverts to savagery, and has to be destroyed; barbarism gathers force at the seaside, as 'enterprising' adults sing along with runically-inscribed Hitler cubs; Konrad, 'dog-paddling', is drowned, and Tulia laments by becoming a dog, in 1933. Hitler fears poisoning, and tightens security at his folksy tea-parties, the dog Harras is poisoned by an 'anarchist'; the Liebenaus are invited to meet the Führer at a reception, but Hitler is engaged in the business of war, and they get to see only his dog. Walter Matern, hitherto an ardent communist, joins the SA, in order to provide Amsel with material for Nazi scarecrows; once a member of the Party, he becomes a fanatical adherent of street-brawling, denouncing his friend, and leading a gang to pulverize him. The logic of events is fractured and unpredictable; individual lives follow strange trajectories that disrupt conventional expectations of sequential plausibility. Jenny Brunies starts life as a gypsy foundling (a story dismissed as a piece of Brunies mystification by Harry and Tulla); weaned on sweets, she is so fat at the age of six that she can barely walk, and has to be conveyed in a pram – until a pantomime-style metamorphosis transforms her into a slim *prima donna* of the ballet. Her toes are blown off by a wartime bomb; this ends her ballet career, and at the novel's close she is a barkeeper, peeing into glasses of lemonade to provide Brauxel with the right mixture for his throat. Her father (a teacher of history!) dies in a concentration camp; the absurd reason that drives him there is that he compulsively devours vitamin tablets that he is supposed to distribute to schoolchildren. Tulla Pokriefke has a miscarriage as a result of jumping too vigorously from a tram; the incongruous consequence is that she becomes a tramconductor. The career of Eddi Amsel is the most fantastical of all; he moves from rural scarecrow-artist to industrial scarecrow-tycoon, the grotesque personification of Germany's post-war economic miracle; in between he adopts an incongruous assortment of roles, with miraculous transitions from devourer of newts' tails – compensatory (like Mahlke!), to make up for his shortcomings on the sportsfield – to the hero of *Faustball*, from fat sweet-devourer to thin chain-smoker, from the Toulouse-Lautrec of the Danzig brothels to the *Kraft durch Freude* ballet master and impresario.

Grass's history is thus manifestly anti-ideological; there are no historical 'laws' to be found in *Dog Years*, no overt or latent sequential logic of events. Events are not determined by the state of the class struggle, or control of the means of production, or the *Weltgeist* manifesting itself through historically-conscious individuals; the only prophet of future developments in the novel is the miller Matern, and his means of foretelling the future (listening to mealworms in a sack of grain) is an appropriately farcical version of ancient Prussian soothsaying – the post-war 'economic miracle' owes its fruition to Matern's tips to industrialists. Grass's gradually evolving commitment to Willy Brandt's gradualist view of history – the 'politics of little steps', which will be seen fully developed in *From the Diary of a Snail* – is glimpsed in humorous form in *Dog Years*: things go one step forward and one back, as one bedwetter at Amsel's school reforms while another relapses: 'While one of the Syck brothers who had been a bedwetter back in the dormitory is able to report a dry bed in the Saskoschin country annex, his brother, hitherto dry, begins to wet his country annex bed regularly and his cot on the porch as well.' (p. 114). In absurd form, there is the principle of 'simultaneous movements, acting as a brake and extinguisher on each other.'[3]

The concept of history as 'absurd process' has a good deal in common with Sartre's 'contingency', and indeed the problems of the individual characters in *Dog Years* in coming to terms with their place in history are expressed in existentialist terms. Grass calls the protagonists of Döblin's novels 'heroes against absurdity'; the characters of *Dog Years* search for an 'authentic' identity in the midst of a radically diseased historical process.

Tulla Pokriefke is a simple case of 'ontic' disorder. The diagnosis follows the lines set out in *Cat and Mouse*: the fundamentally false glamorizing of the German 'destiny', of war and violence as heroic activities (its falsity measured by the 'enterprise' of adults evinced in singing along with Hitler cubs), creates an appetite for excitement that everyday life cannot satisfy; the children of *Dog Years*, like the children of *Cat and Mouse*, experience boredom and disillusionment. On the eve of the outbreak of war, Tulla and Harry play childish games – Doctor and Patient, Stare, Silence – and get bored: 'Now we play the game again, the other way around. Tulla crawls under the wood shavings and I, because she is sick, have to take her temperature with my little finger in her aperture. That too comes to an end. Twice we play stare and don't blink. Tulla wins again. Then because we can't think of any other game, we play silence again.' (*Dog Years*, p. 269). No wonder that Harry Liebenau is later unconcerned about being drafted into the infantry ('It's all one to me. So long as I get out of this lousy burg' – p. 367) or that Tulla can find no more meaningful aspiration than to be pregnant at the first available opportunity. The purposeless spitefulness and violence of Tulla's behaviour – *Dog Years* once more explodes the myth of childhood 'innocence' – is the expression of an empty search for sensations as a substitute for more meaningful personal aims. Tulla denounces Brunies – 'Why? Because.' (p. 303) – is indifferent to the poisoning of Harras – 'Why? Because.' – and wants a baby – 'Why? Because.' The Tulla of *Cat and Mouse* likewise offers her unappetizing body to the schoolboys on the wreck if they find the dead seaman who she is convinced lies in the cabins: they dive, 'not because we really wanted to lay this unfinished little number, but just so . . .' (*Cat and Mouse*, p. 34).

Matern and Amsel are more complex studies of the difficulties of finding meaningful identity in an absurd society. Matern is partially conscious of his fractured personality:

> Yes, I loved him. And they took him away from me. As a boy, I defended him with my fists, for we Materns, all my ancestors, Simon Materna, Gregor Materna, have always protected the weak. But the others were stronger, and I could only look on helplessly as terror broke that voice. Eddi, my Eddi! Since then a lot of things have broken inside me incurably: dissonance, ostracism, shards, fragments of myself, that can never be put together again. (*Dog Years*, p. 419).

But the self-pitying voice here is 'inauthentic'. First, the simple evasions of truth – Matern cannot acknowledge responsibility for betraying Eddi Amsel; the fault is projected onto abstractions, 'they,' 'the others.' Second, the senti-mentalized adulteration of history: Matern romanticizes his Renaissance ancestors into Robin Hoods, proto-communists, heroes of national liberation, and attempts to model his identity on this conception. In reality, they were anarchic plunderers, and the real Matern tradition – 'The Catholicism of the Matern family, as one might expect of a family of millers, was dependent on the wind . . .' (p. 21) – affects Matern's shiftings from one ideology to another in ways that he does not display consciousness of here. Third, there is the suspect ontological jargon, 'dissonance, ostracism, shards', reminding us of one of Matern's idological flirtations with idealist philosophy. The philosophical villains of *Dog Years* are Weininger and Heidegger, and one of the main themes of the novel links the German idealist tradition with the false heroics of Nazism.

'Eddi passed him on to me as a joke.' (p. 168). Heidegger thus enters the consciousness of the grammar-school boys of Danzig in characteristically trivial fashion; Matern, misunderstanding and mistrusting Amsel's irony, takes him up with histrionic seriousness, and plays the role of mentor: 'He was looked upon as strict but fair, admired, and superficially imitated.' (p. 324). Heidegger, thus absorbed by the schoolboys, glamorizes trivialities, exorcising that tedium experienced by all Grass's children in wartime: 'Even in everyday matters philosophical tongues made pre-Socratic leaps, appraising every commonplace incident or object with the tech sergeant's painstakingly acquired knowledge. Underdone potatoes in their jackets . . . were called "spuds forgetful of Being." . . . The daily facts of life in an AA battery, such as semi-serious disciplinary drill, tedious practice alerts, or greasy-messy rifle cleaning, were disposed of with an expression overheard from the tech sergeant: "After all, the essence of being-there is its existence." ' (p. 324). The jargon provides them with a spurious sense of personal identity and significance – even Tulla's search for authentication through pregnancy is given a Heideggerish tinge: '. . . she hobbled into the dunes between the tech sergeant and Air Force auxiliary Störtebeker in the hope that they would both make her a baby; but tech sergeant and Air Force auxiliary preferred to indulge in other proofs of existence: they shot dune rabbits.' (p. 325). Störtebeker, ironically named after the leader of a medieval pirate gang, adopts pseudo-heroic pretensions, prefacing sentences with 'I, as a pre-Socratic', parroting Heidegger's Nietzschean primitivism.

Eddi Amsel's flirtations with ontology are naturally enough of a more subtle nature. Weininger,[4] the anti-semitic Jew who became a convert to Protestantism and killed himself in self-disgust, offers him no heroic fillip to identity; on the contrary, he offers a racial myth of the Jew as the 'feminine' principle, formless, passive, unheroic, identityless: '. . . things that will forever be beyond the reach of the authentic Jew: spontaneous being, divine right, the oak tree, the trumpet, the Siegfried motif, self-creation, the words: ' "I am" ' (p. 187). The novel suggests that Weininger's concept of the Jew is the opposite side of the Heidegger coin; the perspective is the same, the heroic idealization of the Aryan spirit, the identification of the Jew with the merely material principle. Eddi Amsel seems to recognize himself in aspects of Weininger's characterization of the Jewish mentality: 'they believe in nothing, because they *are* nothing and for that very reason they can become anything they please . . . because they are neither fearful nor brave, because they are unheroic and never anything but ironic . . .' (p. 204). Under the influence of Weininger his art deteriorates, and only sparrows deign to be scared by his scarecrows.

But Amsel, the central ironic voice of the novel, does not remain fixed in a naive faith in Weininger's biological mysticism. He seems to be aware of Weininger's masochistic paradoxes; if the essence of the Jewish spirit is ironic and skeptical, then it can no more believe in Weininger's portrait than in any other. Amsel shows this awareness by working on a scarecrow of Weininger in SA uniform; the results are 'unsatisfactory' of course because the model hasn't got the right 'Aryan essence'.

The conception of Amsel in *Dog Years* is a critical confrontation of notions of individual or racial 'essence'. He is described as 'the most restless hero' in the novel ('*beweglich*' also means 'fluid' or 'flexible') (p. 32); the deliberate and rapid succession of roles that he adopts is perhaps the only 'authentic' existential stance that the novel displays. The flexibility and prolixity of personalities in Amsel is a conscious response to the 'absurdity' of history; what ties them together is a keen responsiveness to the pluralist complexity of reality. The success of his scarecrows depends upon his minute and particular attention to detail: 'It was Eddi Amsel's keen sense of reality in all its innumerable forms, the curious eye surmounting his plump cheek, which provided his products with closely observed detail, which made them functional and crow-repellent.' (p. 39). Amsel deals not in abstract categories, like Heidegger or Weininger, but in the minute discrimination of individual traits: 'What no bird expert can do, Amsel could: he was able to distinguish as individuals the members of a crowd bevy congress of sparrows, whom everybody believes to be equally colourless.' (p. 200). He stands in the middle of events, ironic, humorous, detached; when the humorless Matern asks him why he doesn't create idealistic SA men as well as brutish ones he replies 'that precisely this had been his artistic purpose, that he hadn't intended criticism of any kind, but merely wished, through his art, to create a hodgepodge of good guys and bastards, after the manner of life itself.' (p. 217).

Amsel is thus the appropriate Jewish-liberal hero of a liberal, anti-ideological novel. Though its conception of history is fundamentally a materialist one, it rigorously combats theoretical orderings of the material of history; for Grass the concreteness of history can be realized only through the exhaustive inventory of separate details. It is no accident that Amsel, like Oskar, is the son of a shopkeeper.

The language of *Dog Years* demands special attention. Brauxel suggests one reason why, as he introduces Eddi Amsel's diary: 'Brauksel holds that there isn't much point in reproducing here the broad island idiom written by Eduard Amsel as an eight-year-old schoolboy; in the present narrative it will be possible at most to record in direct discourse the charms of this language, which will soon die out with the refugee's associations and once dead may prove to be of interest to science in very much the same way as Latin.' (p. 54).

The irony here is transparent, for the novel as a whole is dedicated to the preservation of decaying language. Besides attempting to refresh the German memory of the past, it attempts to resurrect scraps of this history of the German language.

Thus we find for instance, particularly in the narrative of Harry Liebenau, a constant attention to etymologies, the origins of phrases, names and expressions. Liebenau discusses the origin of 'Koshnavia', dismissing the theory that it is connected with rebellious '*Kopfschneider*' (head cutters), preferring the view that it descends from the Polish administrator Koznewski. He delves into the origin of Tulla's mother's family name, into the Polish root of the German village Osterwick, and produces specimens of Koshnavian speech; elsewhere, the origin of the anti-semitic slang-word '*Sheeny*' ('Itzig') is unearthed. Brauxel adopts similar precision, telling us that the natives of the Vistula delta called stones '*Zellacken*', and proving it with a list of examples. This painstaking attention to local details of the history of language is a paradigm of the novel's attempt to realize the concreteness of the past.

'There is no contradiction between playfulness and pedantry; the one brings on the other.' (p. 9). Brauxel offers on the first page of the novel a justification for the orgies of specialized terminologies that punctuate the novel. Some of them at least support his assertion, the Rabelaisian catalogue of expressions for gonorrhea, for instance:

> Wherever the two of them, master and dog, set their six feet, whether on the rugged Alb, on East Frisian marshland, or in the destitute villages of the Westerwald, everywhere the clap has a different name: here they say dripping Johnny, there they warn against lovesnot; here they count candledrops, there they tell of snipe honey; goldenrod and his lordship's cold, widow's tears and pistachio oil are pithy regional terms, as are cavalryman

and runner; Matern calls it 'the milk of vengeance.'
(*Dog Years*, p. 422).

This wealth of local variants is intended to testify to the
vitality of the German language – and of gonorrhea; Matern's
addition to the list demonstrates the process of language
ceaselessly creating new forms. Likewise there are huge lists
of specialized terms of geological forms, for milling, for
ballet steps; Grass exhibits a delight in these names, as if the
specificity of their referents rendered them more truthful, less
arbitrary than other, more abstract verbal signs.

The novel is not only concerned to preserve dialect; it takes
equal pains with the language of the Third Reich. The
materials of a social history of Nazi speech are contained in
Grass's writings, and in *Dog Years* this accuracy of notation
has specific point, since the language of ex-Nazis after the war
betrays the habits of thought they have conveniently chosen
to forget. Hauptbannführer Uli Göpfert reminisces about a
Hitler birthday ritual in Danzig and remembers that it had
been 'Führerweather' (a sentimental Nazi term for 'lovely
day': 'The sun shining out of a cloudless sky on the gable roofs
of Nuremberg during the week of the annual Party rally was
popularly described as "Führerweather" ').[5] Inge feels like
copulating with Matern on a roadside, and unconsciously
slips into *Blubo* language: 'I'd do it with you right here in the
open, day and night, under the open sky, in the bosom of
nature . . .' (p. 411). The language of Nazi officialdom is
faithfully transmitted, together with its comic aspects: the
Liebenaus receive a stud certificate describing Harras's mating
performance, singling out for praise his eugenic '*Deckfreudig-
keit*' ('mating joyfulness' – Harry Liebenau is not allowed to
use the word when he recounts the story in his primary school.)
Less amusingly, concentration camps enter popular usage, the
name Stutthof being used for vague threats and menaces:

That little word took on more and more meaning. 'Hey,
you! You got a yen for Stutthof?' – 'If you don't keep

that trap of yours shut, you'll end up in Stutthof.' A
sinister word had moved into apartment houses, went
upstairs and downstairs, sat at kitchen tables, was
supposed to be a joke, and some actually laughed:
'They're making soap in Stutthof now, it makes you
want to stop washing.' (*Dog Years*, p. 294).

The pervasive post-war claim of innocence – 'we never knew
about what went on in the concentration camps' – is countered
with the evidence of language.

Stutthof here enters the mythology of the language (to be
blotted out again, of course, when post-war memories start to
fail); this piece of social history conveys Grass's essentially
dynamic understanding and use of the creative possibilities
of language. The momentum of *Dog Years* is sustained
(despite occasional flagging) by linguistic inventiveness,
words opening up new relationships to other words through
association, punning, sound similarities. Razor blades provide
the metaphor for Brauxel's dislike of them: 'Brauxel has an
unblunting distaste for unused razor blades.'(p. 82). Hedwig
Lau is associated with the train in which she travels to school,
so that her physique is transferred to it: 'Was it not unseemly
that the narrow-chested narrow-gauge locomotive should
chug away regardless of Hedwig Lau's absence?' (p. 81). Why
did the Gutenberg monument get put up in the Jäschkental
Forest? Purely verbal associations provide one pseudo-
explanation, based on the similarity between '*Buch*' ('book')
'*Buche*' ('beech'): 'or else they chose the forest, because
Jäschkental Forest was a beech wood and Gutenberg, before
casting metal type, had carved the letters he printed his
books with out of beech wood.' (p. 225–6; '*Gutenberg . . .
Buchstaben aus Buchenholz für den Buchdruck geschnitzt
hatte.*') A cascade of punning associations is generated from
the word 'brown', as Harry Liebenau attempts to drum up the
flavour of Nazi uniforms: '. . . shit brown, at best clay brown,
sodden, pasty, Party brown, SA brown, the brown of all

Brown Books, Brown Houses, Braunau brown, Eva Braun, uniform brown, a far cry from khaki, the brown shat on white plates by a thousand pimply asses, brown derived from split peas and sausages . . .' (p. 215; Manheims's translation skilfully bolsters the puns with half-rhymes like 'far cry/ khaki').

This verbal inventiveness is presented as a kind of moral value in the novel. Dr Brunies challenges the inventiveness of his students, setting them 'absurd' composition topics like, 'the destinies of a tin can' or: 'When I was a cough drop, growing smaller and smaller in a little girl's mouth' – the kind of objects lovingly described in Grass's prose. Only a few of them are equal to the task: 'Apparently his idea was to feed our imaginations, and since out of forty students two can reasonably be expected to have an imagination, thirty eight thirds were permitted to doze while two– another and myself – unrolled the destinies of the tin can, thought up original marriage customs for the Zulus, and spied on a cough drop growing smaller in a little girl's mouth.' (p. 300). Brauxel exhorts the customers of Jenny's bar to make up stories about anything and everything: 'More stories. More stories. Keep going! As long as we're telling stories, we're alive. As long as stories keep coming, with or without a point, dog stories, eel stories, scarecrow stories, rat stories, flood stories, recipe stories, stories full of lies and schoolbook stories, as long as stories have power to entertain us, no hell can take us in. Your turn, Walter. Tell stories as long as you love your life.' (p. 575).

It's as though Grass's ontological formula were: 'I write, therefore I am.' Narration preserves history from oblivion, resurrecting the concrete past as the context of individual lives. The dynamic process of inventing new verbal forms, forging new connections in language, is a kind of mirror of the historical process; if history is 'absurd' and illogical, it is therefore not inevitable or 'necessary', but open to change and redirection. This is the meaning, I think, of the 'Rabelaisian' elements in Grass's work, so often noted by critics; Bakhtin,

writing on Rabelais, puts it most memorably: 'It is as if
words had been released from the shackles of sense, to enjoy a
play period of complete freedom and establish unusual
relationships among themselves. True, no new consistent
links are formed in most cases, but the brief coexistence of
these words, expressions, and objects outside the usual logical
conditions discloses their inherent ambivalence. Their multiple meanings and the potentialities that would not manifest
themselves in normal conditions are revealed.'[6]

The baroque prolixity of symbolic patterns in *Dog Years* is
also generated from verbal association. The title itself may be
associatively derived from 'dog-days' (*Hundstage*), the mid-
summer period when the dogstar shines and the heat is at its
fiercest – and in *Dog Years* the prevailing temperature is
'hotter than hell'! The two main images, dog and scarecrow,
both depend upon a complementary blurring of normal
logical distinctions, between humans and animals on the one
hand and between humans and inanimate effigies on the other.
And the other images clustered around these totems can be
plotted as associative chains – dog: guardian of hell: hell
fires: apocalypse; the underworld: mines: hideaways; scarecrows: machines: mining; dog: blackness: blackbird (*Amsel*):
scarecrows, etc. Punning connections abound – for instance,
the chapters of the first narrative bear the strange name (the
influence comes from Jean Paul) of '*Frühschichten*', meaning
both 'morning shifts' and 'early layers', the beginnings of
Amsel and Matern. And '*Schichten*' (layers) will take us to
Brunies' geological specimens and the '*geschichtet*' pile of
bones, if we want it to.
   This associative casualness of image-formation declares the
fundamental playfulness and nonseriousness of the 'symbols'
of *Dog Years*. This doesn't mean, as Wiegenstein and others
have taken it to mean,[7] that the novel is a formalist work, an
autonomous structure of language reflecting only itself rather
than anything 'outside' the novel. Rather, Grass adopts the

same oblique, distancing approach to reality that he had chosen to follow in *The Tin Drum*, preferring the role of deceptive pandar to symbolic tastes rather than that of the naively chaste realist. For Grass, the novel is 'the whore among arts.'[8]

Thus Brauxel's first symbolic scenario of hell – the burnt goose at the Matern mill – is immediately followed by aesthetic self-questioning: 'Brauxel wonders whether he may not have put too much diabolical display into his account of Grandmother Matern's resurrection . . . was it necessary to have her puff steam and spit fire?' (*Dog Years*, p. 28). This deliberate stressing of the artificiality of the previous scene is designed to create unease, as is Harry Liebenau's skepticism about the mine-symbol: 'He owns a mine between Hildesheim and Sarstedt. Or maybe the whole thing is sculduggery camouflage fifth column, even if his name is Brauxel Brauksel Brauchsel.' (pp. 321–2). As soon as we ask a question like 'what does this symbol mean?', the novel replies with a deflationary sarcasm – about the significance of Brauxel's apocalyptic date 4 February, 1962, for instance: 'On the fourth of February of this year, as Brauxel has read in a number of newspaper articles, this world is expected to end . . .' (pp. 101–102; in the German, Brauxel has read this in '*feuilletons*' [arts pages] – and Grass has recorded his loathing of West German *feuilletons* on several occasions!) Harry Liebenau refers to Brauxel's apocalypse as that 'Applesauce with the stars.' (p. 180) applesauce = '*Quatsch*', nonsense.

'So the novel is a piece of cynicism,' the reader may conclude. Cunningly, Grass plants such responses to Brauxel/ Amsel's art in the novel, to disconcerting effect; thus the serious minded Walter Matern is not amused during his tour of the scarecrow mine: 'Matern, the stranger below, pronounces this brand of humour too cynical for his taste. To his mind, humour should have a liberating, healing, even a saving effect.' (p. 592). Unfortunately and unconsciously, Walter

Matern echoes the responses of the Nazi censors who ban
Amsel's ballet *The Scarecrows*: 'In general, they thought the
latter part of the story too sinister and allusive. The life-
affirming element was absent, and the two gentlemen declared
in unison: "Soldiers at the front want something gay, not
some gloomy rumbling underworld."' (p. 363). We remember,
too, that Weininger characterizes the Jewish mentality as
ironically cynical. So is *Dog Years* a piece of degenerate
Jewish art . . . ? The novel's 'cynicism' is strategic, designed
to make normative responses untenable.

Like *The Tin Drum*, *Dog Years* is harshly satiric of the
aestheticizing of reality. As the war breaks out, Harry
Liebenau borrows a spyglass and goes up on the roof to
watch the bombing (like Matzerath at the fall of Danzig):
'The war looked phony and disappointing. . . . Maybe they're
out playing and school will start again tomorrow.' (p. 271).
Four months out of a French prison camp, Captain Hufnagel
goes to the theatre to see Borchert's *Draussen vor der Tür*, a
nightmarish account of a soldier's return from the Russian
front; his account is already in the style of *feuilleton*:
'Excellent play, incidentally. Took the whole family to see it
in Hagen, pathetic little theatre. Goes straight to the heart.
Weren't you a professional actor? What a part that would be
for you. That Borchert hits the nail on the head. Haven't we
all of us been through it, myself too? Didn't we all become
strangers to ourselves and our loved ones while we were out
there at the front?' (p. 414). At the novel's close, Matern is
puzzled by Amsel's story of the boy who threw away a penknife;
as soon as he decided that it's all a piece of symbolism, 'the
story oppresses him less.' (p. 566).

At moments, the novel abandons its obliqueness of
approach and addresses reality directly. Thus, the impact of
war on Harry Liebenau firsthand is to make him give up his
aestheticism and write hard, factual prose: 'No more poems
written with adolescent sperm and heart's blood.' Once the
screaming of that shed had splattered his ears like birdshot,

his diary is restricted to simple sentences: 'The gun backs into the glass shed. War is more boring than school. Everybody's waiting for miracle weapons. After the war I'm going to see lots of movies. Yesterday I saw my first dead man. . . . Löns and Heidegger are wrong about lots of things.' (p. 372). And at one point Grass drops the Döblin mask, the artist hidden behind his creation, and speaks out about what is on his mind, why the preservation of historical reality is so vital – as Harry confesses to falsifying Stutthof: 'With the help of these models (Heidegger and Co) he succeeded in burying a real mound made of human bones under medieval allegories. The pile of bones, which in reality cried out to high heaven between Troyl and Kaiserhafen, was mentioned in his diary as a place of sacrifice, erected in order that purity might come-to-be in the luminous, which transluminates purity and fosters light.' (pp. 338–9).

NOTES

1. The quotations in this paragraph are taken from 'Über meinen Lehrer Döblin. Rede zum 10. Todestag Döblins', *Akzente* XIV (1967), 290–309.
2. George Steiner, 'A note on Günter Grass' in *Language and Silence* (Harmondsworth: Penguin Books, 1969), p. 158.
3. *Akzente* XIV, 291.
4. There is a good study of Weininger's influence on *Dog Years*: Wesley V. Blomster's 'The Documentation of a Novel: Otto Weininger and *Hundejahre* by Günter Grass,' *Monatshefte* LXI (1969), 122–138.
5. Grunberger, p. 116.
6. Bakhtin, p. 423.
7. See Roland Wiegenstein in Loschütz, pp. 78–9.
8. *Text und Kritik* 1/1a, 1.

THE POET

The next two chapters cover aspects of Grass's career as a writer that are relatively little known or appreciated. In approaching Grass as a poet and as a dramatist, it is extremely difficult to forget that Grass has gained pre-eminent recognition as a novelist: in what follows I have not attempted to do so. Certainly the most immediate kind of interest that these works are likely to arouse for admirers of Grass's novels lies in the large number of parallels or anticipations of images and themes explored in the prose works. Standing by themselves, they would not have made Grass a significant contemporary writer – the body of lyric writing is too slender, the dramatic productions too flawed.

Still, the reader of the poems and plays encounters a good deal of illumination or arresting confirmation of some central tendencies in Grass's work, and some writing of high quality. My own satisfaction in reading these works comes chiefly from the discovery of how closely Grass's work – even when it is at its most 'absurd' – reflects contemporary social and psychological realities. Political themes are apparent from the very start, and while the poems and plays, like the work in general, display a clear development in the direction of increasingly overt political subject-matter, the gain in directness often entails a loss in effectiveness. Certainly in the case of the poems, it seems to me that the most powerful political statements are made through the medium of a symbolic language.

The poems have recently gained a small but influential body of admirers in Germany, and it seems likely that serious study of them will increase. The plays also have their

champions, but by and large they fail to convince. I have
tried to make out the case for one or two of the early plays,
and for the fascinating and infuriating play about Brecht, *The
Plebeians Rehearse the Uprising*. But I think Grass rarely
shows a full appreciation of the problems of dramatic writing,
and it is in studying these works that one comes to the
conclusion that Grass's special gift is for narration.

'. . . Lyric poetry has always offered me the chance or
opportunity of taking stock, of putting myself in most
particular question.' Grass's familiar existentialist phrasing
of the 'challenge' of lyric poetry suggests the difficulty of
assessing his poetic output – contained in three volumes published between 1956 and 1967 and collected in the Luchterhand *Gesammelte Gedichte* (*Collected Poems*) – in isolation
from the work as a whole or more latterly, from his political
involvements. The reader confronts a writer with very little
interest in the 'purity' of literary genres[2] and a great deal of
expressed mistrust or even contempt for 'formalist' writing.
In 1960, Grass made a witty contribution to a conference of
poets in Berlin, declaring himself an 'occasional poet' rather
than a 'laboratory poet', describing with evident ironic relish
his eccentric rituals for composing poetry:

> As soon as I get the feeling that there's a poem in the air
> again, I strictly avoid eating anything with a pod or a
> shell, and sally forth, even though it costs me a bit, on
> meaningless meaningful taxi-rides, so that that poem in
> the air shakes itself loose . . . But when there's a poem in
> the air, and I suspect that this time she, I mean the Muse,
> is going to visit me with something in five strophes of
> three lines each, neither the avoidance of things in pods
> or incontinent taxi-riding is of any use, then there's only
> one thing: to buy some fresh herrings, take them out,
> cook them, put them in vinegar, turn down invitations
> from people who like to talk about electronic music, go

instead to parties where professors intrigue and listen to intrigue, but heavens above! not to take a taxi home, but to go to bed and sleep without a pillow. Admittedly this method doesn't always work. Once I must confess that the diametrical opposite – I bought half a pig's head, made pork brawn, talked to people about electronic music, kept out of the way of professors and their intrigues, slept with two pillows – provided me with a poem in five strophes of three lines each which has since become part of literary history.[3]

When one looks at some of the fruits of this method of composition, they seem incongruous with their declared origins. Here is a poem 'in five strophes of three lines each', from the volume *Gleisdreieck* (*Triangle Junction*), published in 1960:

Adebar

Einst stand hier vieles auf dem Halm,
und auf Kaminen standen Störche;
dem Leib entfiel das fünfte Kind.

Lang wusst ich nicht, dass es noch Störche gibt,
dass ein Kamin, der rauchlos ist,
den Störchen Fingerzeig bedeutet.

Tot die Fabrik, doch oben halbstark Störche;
sie sind der Rauch, der weiss mit roten Beinen
auf feuchten Wiesen niederschlägt.

Einst rauchte in Treblinka sonntags
viel Fleisch, das Adebar gesegnet,
liess, Heissluft, einen Segelflieger steigen.

Das war in Polen, wo die Jungfrau
Maria steif auf Störchen reitet,
doch – wenn der Halm fällt – nach Agypten flieht.

Gesammelte Gedichte (p. 77).

Stork

Once there stood here plenty on the stalk
And storks stood on the chimneys;
The fifth child slipped from out of the womb.

For ages, I didn't know storks still exist,
Or that a smokeless chimney means
A pointed finger to a stork.

Dead the factory, yet above, young storks;
They are the smoke, white with red legs
That settles on moist meadows.

Once at Treblinka on a Sunday
Plenty of flesh was smoked and blessed by storks
Hot air that helped the gliders to rise.

That was in Poland, where the Virgin
Mary rides stiffly on storks,
Yet – when the stalk falls – flees to Egypt.)[4]

This poem has a tautness and precision to arrest professional intrigues. Its powerful effect is dependent on formal concentration: the easy, fertile normality of the first stanza, in which children 'slip' from the womb, is conveyed by means of rhythmical regularity and metrical smoothness, and buttressed by repetition and internal rhyming ('*stand . . . standen*', '*vieles . . . entfiel*'). The introduction of Treblinka is accompanied with a disruption of metrical and syntactical pattern – the word 'dead' pushed to the beginning of the line, contrasting as sharply as possible with the atmosphere evoked in stanza one. Yet the full shock is held in reserve: Treblinka is a ghastly parody of normality; there is still 'plenty of flesh' (*viel Fleisch*), storks still land on the chimney and procreate. The play of tenses – normality pushed into the remote past, Treblinka also once-upon-a-time but simultaneously presented in the present tense – is part of the strategy to suggest how the

monstrous becomes part of everyday life, how equally the
present 'normality' cannot be sharply separated from the past.
Everything in the poem depends upon restraint – even the
accusatory 'pointed finger' is couched ambiguously ('*Fingerzeig*' also means simply 'indication' or 'signpost') and the
storks settle on it as a familiar object from their optical
perspective.

Grass is an uneven poet, and only a percentage of his
poems are of the quality of 'Adebar'. Yet the image of the
'occasional poet' he projects in the 1960 speech and elsewhere, of the casual, absurdist eccentric dependent on quirky
flashes of inspiration, is I think a pose, misleading if it
suggests that Grass's approach to poetic form and language
is casual and naive. There are plenty of careless lines and some
careless poems in *Gesammelte Gedichte*, but they suggest
lapses of concentration rather than a fundamental indifference
to poetic form.

Grass's first volume of poems, *Die Vorzüge der Windhühner* (*The Advantages of Windfowl*), which appeared in
1956 (it was also his first substantial appearance as a writer),
declares its surrealist playfulness in its title. What are 'windfowl?' How can they be said to have 'advantages'? Over what?
The title-poem is a pseudo-logical structure consisting of
answers to these questions:

> Weil sie kaum Platz einnehmen
> auf ihrer Stange aus Zugluft
> und nicht nach meinen zahmen Stühlen picken.
> Weil sie die harten Traumrinden nicht verschmähen,
> nicht den Buchstaben nachlaufen,
> die der Briefträger jeden Morgen vor meiner Tür
> 　　verliert.
> Weil sie stehen bleiben,
> von der Brust bis zur Fahne
> eine duldsame Fläche, ganz klein beschrieben,
> kein Feder vergessen, kein Apostroph . . .

Weil sie die Tür offen lassen,
der Schlüssel die Allegorie bleibt,
die dann und wann kräht.
Weil ihre Eier so leicht sind
und bekömmlich, durchsichtig.

Weil diese Stille so weich ist,
das Fleisch am Kinn einer Venus
nähre ich sie. –

Gesammelte Gedichte, (p. 19).

Because they hardly take up space
On their perch of air current,
And do not peck at my tame chairs.
Because they do not despise the dreams' hard rinds,
Do not run for the alphabet
That the postman loses every morning at my door.
Because they stand still,
From the breast to the tail,
A patient surface in very small writing,
No feather forgotten, no apostrophe . . .
Because they leave the door open,
To which the key is allegory,
Which crows now and then.
Because their eggs are so light
And digestible, transparent.

Because this silence is so soft,
Flesh on the chin of Venus,
I feed it. –

There is awkwardness and self-consciousness here – the
'rinds of dreams' are predictably hard, and the 'key of
allegory', even if it's a joke cliché, is a ponderous one – but
little to suggest indifference to poetic form. Grass follows
modernist masters (like Pound and Eliot, for English readers)

in using syntactic pattern and repetition as the bolster of free verse ('Because they . . . Because they', 'do not . . .do not'), in supporting this structure through assonance (*'Weil ihre Eier so leicht sind . . . Weil diese Stille so weich ist,/ das Fleisch am Kinn . . .'*). This shapely syntactical clarity liberates metaphor from the need to respect normal logical categories, dissolves mental props like 'tenor' and 'vehicle', so that the birds are both feeders and food, both perceivers and perceived, both the objects that the poem describes and that description itself (*'Feder'* provides a pun, meaning both 'feather' and 'pen'). The line of poetic descent, from Symbolism via Surrealism, is manifest.

These images provide an introduction to the mythological system of the volume (well described in Wieser's book), a network of recurrent associations that provides the larger unifying structure of the poems. The central image is the house: there the poet sits in a 'tame chair' in his room, working at his desk with drawings and poems. Around him, the everyday objects of a domestic interior: furniture, clothes, writing implements. The poems touch frequently on domestic supplies as well – gas, heat and lighting, above all on food and the indispensible gas cooker. The apparently prosaic 'tameness' of these objects belies their capacity to behave in strange and disturbing ways: in the poem 'Open Wardrobe', for instance, the contents of a wardrobe have an animistic vitality that seems to have been absorbed from their wearers.[5] 'The white balls asleep in the pockets/dream of moths . . .',, 'in this belt the snake grows weary.' – the wood itself seems to be endowed with life, whilst the inhabitants of the house are imagined as dead:

> Before the wardrobe falls silent, turns into wood,
> a distant relation of pine-trees –
> who will wear the coat
> one day when you're dead?

> (*Poems of Günter Grass*, p. 18)

Outside, meanwhile, is a garden and a park, whose contents the poet observes: human scenes, boys playing football, people walking across a path or a square; but above all, the spectacles of nature, the flight of birds, the growth and decline of plants, the succession of the seasons, and especially the weather. Many of the poems deal with violent weather, threatening the security of the domestic interior: there are floods, high winds, plentiful snow, extreme heat and a plague of mosquitoes. In between, as a kind of protective boundary, there is the window with its blinds, or the garden-fence. Watching the windfowl, 'I lean happily on the fence.'

Wieser informs us that many of these details reflect Grass's surroundings as he wrote the poems in the fifties, he was living at that time in a romantically bomb-scarred villa in the Grunewald district of Berlin, a house with a large garden facing a park where boys played football and where the pond was apparently infested with mosquitoes in the summer. Yet there is a more general 'objective correlative' to the poems; they reflect the conditions of life in Germany in the immediate post-war years, when food, clothing, electricity and gas were matters of vital concern, and indeed liable to interruption: 'We remember this time: it was short of cabbages, potatoes and calories, but long on power cuts and intense discussions.' (*Über das Selbstverständliche* p. 58). In addition, many of the poems carry Grass's common mythic structuring of recent German history – an idyllic beginning, set in the distant past, is rudely shattered by calamity, and then follows a period of flight and retreat into protective corners from which the lyric subject observes the chaos outside. There is an overall ironic perspective that resembles the novels to follow: the poet's imagery effects a 'making strange' of the familiar objects of everyday life, mocking that desired bourgeois safety and comfort that is designed to separate the interior world of the house from the fearsome forces of nature or history outside. He uses himself as exemplary subject.

Read in this way, the poems of this volume form a coherent sequence with clear affinities to *The Tin Drum*. The presence of related images – glass-shattering voices, dwarfs, hunchbacks, Polish flags and hairy triangles – is not in itself as significant as the desire to combine these images into something like a coherent narrative. Perhaps Gottfried Benn was right when in 1953 he advised the author of these poems to turn to prose, and Grass may have acknowledged the wisdom of this advice when he published some of the poems separately under the title *Short Stories from Berlin*. The narrative tricks of *The Tin Drum* are often to be glimpsed – that initial gambit of involving the reader, for instance, by putting in his mouth a question about the advantages of windfowl and then proceeding to answer it, anticipates the first chapter of the novel (which is obviously more aggressive in its way of grasping our attention). Yet the most obviously narrative poems in the collection are those set in the form of parables, which suggest once again that Grass was not altogether immune to the Kafkaesque fashions of German writing in the fifties. Representative of these is 'The Flood', and it is characteristic that Grass used its material as the basis of a play:

> We are waiting for the rain to stop,
> although we have got accustomed
> to standing behind the curtain, being invisible,
> Spoons have become sieves, nobody dares now
> to stretch a hand out.
> Many things are floating in the streets,
> things people carefully hid in the dry time.
> How awkward to see your neighbour's stale old beds.
> Often we stand by the water-gauge
> and compare our worries like watches.
> Some things can be regulated.
> But when the butts overflow, the inherited cup fills,
> we shall have to pray.

The cellar is submerged, we brought the crates up
and are checking their contents against the list.
So far nothing has been lost.
Because the water is now certain to drop soon,
we have begun to sew sunshades.
It will be difficult to cross the square once more,
distinct, with a shadow heavy as lead.
We shall miss the curtain at first,
and go into the cellar often
to consider the mark
which the water bequeathed us.

(*Poems of Günter Grass* p. 19)

This is a rather uninspired attempt at a Kafka parable, its symbolic overtones are too bald – the 'inherited cup' and 'stale old beds' seem perilously close to clichéd Nazi skeletons-in-the-cupboard – and its language inert at times ('comparing our worries like watches' is a classically stale simile-trouvaille.) But the urge to narrate, to lay out a large spatial and temporal canvas is unmistakeable, and it carries images whose implications are worked out in the whole volume – objects 'made strange', machines that don't work, curtains that shield intrusions from the outside, catalogues of the past.

A more successful venture in the same mode is the poem that closes the collection – 'Blechmusik' (Music for Brass), its title particularly prophetic of *Die Blechtrommel*. It carries the historical myth refined in 'Adebar' – an idyllic past in the womb of a trumpet (Oskar's grandmother's skirts come to mind) is disrupted through an obviously military blast on that instrument. The familiar world is made strange and monstrous:

Today I don't know who woke us,
disguised as flowers in vases,
or else in sugar bowls . . .

(*Poems of Günter Grass*, p. 28)

Yet the 'we' of the poem look for some refuge, the equivalent
of Oskar's hospital bed with its rails and door to ward off
intrusions:

> Now we're on the run and our luggage with us.
> All half-empty paper bags, every crater in our beer,
> cast-off coats, clocks that have stopped,
> graves paid for by other people,
> and women very short of time,
> for a while we fill them.

The flight of Mary into Egypt again; the dominant significance of the image of the house in these poems reflects the
predicament of the refugee driven from Danzig, whose
substitute homes can never provide security.

Grass's second collection of poems, *Gleisdreieck* (*Triangle
Junction*), which appeared a year later than *The Tin Drum*,
seems to me his finest. The concrete realities that the poems
address, reflected only through the code of associative images
in *The Advantages of Windfowl*, now moves forward into
prominent focus; the title refers to a Berlin underground
station where lines from the two sectors of the city form a
triangular junction. Buildings are going up, built over the
rubble of war-damage – this is now the Berlin of the somewhat belated post-war reconstruction; with a kind of
remarkable prophetic insight in pre-wall Berlin, the opening
poem ('five strophes of three lines each') concerns the building
of 'fire-proof walls'. These are associated with a kind of white-
washing: they are 'immaculately sawn out', one of them
carries Persil advertisements, a boy rueing the loss of his
rubble-playground throws a snowball (*Gesammelte Gedichte*,
p. 76). In a fine parable-style poem with a Brechtian title, 'The
Ballad of the Black Cloud', the builders leave behind lime,
which is eaten to good effect by an 'immaculate' hen who lays
her brood in the builder's sand; the black cloud is an ironic

apocalypse threatening the security of the brood in the sand,
but passing by – not without disturbing effect:

> And no-one will ever be sure
> What came of those four eggs
> Under the hen, under the cloud,
>
> What happened to them in the builders' sand.

(p. 96).

In another powerful conception, 'The Great Rubble Lady
Speaks', the lament of the rubble lady is drowned by the
sentimental sounds of a *Biedermeier* society comfortably
reinstalled:

> But all the stations, here and over there,
> Broadcast from morning to night only that
> Shit-ridden old waltz king.

(p. 156)

The poetic persona of these poems, however, registers the
hollowness of this return to 'normality', the secret anxieties
that it attempts to mask and suppress. The everyday world
opens up sudden chasms of anxiety: in the poem 'Friday' for
instance, the poet brings home fresh herrings to cook (the
poem takes as its subject the ritual of composing a poem),
unwraps them from their newspaper-wrapping, only to find
that the newspaper contains news of crisis and disaster. In
one of the finest poems in this volume, where Grass is at the
peak of his powers, each everyday object or action becomes
strange and monstrous:

Saturn

> In this big house –
> from the rats
> who know about the drains,

to the pigeons
who know nothing –
I live and suppose much.

Came home late,
opened the house
with my key
and noticed as I hunted for my key
that I needed a key
to enter my own home.

Was quite hungry
ate a chicken
with my hands
and noticed as I ate the chicken
that I was eating a chicken
which was cold and dead.

Then stooped,
took off both shoes
and noticed as I took off my shoes
that we have to stoop
if we want to take
shoes off.

I lay horizontal,
smoked the cigarette,
and in the darkness was certain
that someone held out his open hand
when I knocked the ashes
from my cigarette.

At night Saturn comes
and holds out his hand.
With my ashes, he
cleans his teeth, Saturn.
we shall climb
into his jaws.

(*Poems of Günter Grass* pp. 43–4)

Once more, the poem's formal structure is tight and econo-
mical, setting up a pattern of expectations and working
variations upon it (the influence of Brecht is again apparent).
Each stanza except the last consists of a single sentence,
pivoting around a verb expressing perception ('suppose much
. . . noticed . . . noticed . . . noticed. . . . was certain'). Simple
repetitions flank the main verb, which acts to *transform* the
object of perception: the key that is repeated in the second
half of stanza two is not the same 'normal' key that appears
before the verb, and so on. The tension escalates: the last
more emphatic 'was certain' leads to the most fantastic of the
transformations, of an ashtray into the cannibal god of
melancholy. This brilliant image fuses together everything
that precedes. The opposition of height and depth, light and
darkness, rat and pigeon is a recurrent structural pattern of
Grass's imagination;[6] the fake pigeon or dove, symbol of
peace (cf. Oskar, *The Tin Drum*, p. 99: 'I would sooner
entrust a message of peace to a hawk or a vulture than to a
dove . . .'), settling on the roof like the storks on chimneys, is
exploded in the image of grey cigarette-ash, the grey planet,
the not-so-pearly teeth. The imagery of food (the cold
chicken that suddenly appears monstrous) culminates in the
god who devours his children. The stoop to untie the shoes is
both a counterpart of the 'climb' into Saturn's jaws and a
gesture symbolic of the engulfing melancholy. The nervous,
cigarette-smoking poetic persona does indeed 'put itself in
question' in poems like 'Saturn'.

The stress on that word 'noticed' in the poem highlights the
importance of visual imagination to Grass: the poems of
Gleisdreieck frequently create an optic in which the objects of
everyday life are seen afresh, confronting 'automatic perception' with the grotesque realities of alternative perspectives.
This is seen at its most obvious in poems like 'Fog', where
atmospheric conditions make Berlin's newly-restored 'normality' look precarious and insecure:

Surprises too:
Where previously the opera stood firm
There appears with chill lights
The ship Titanic.

(Gesammelte Gedichte, p.134)

The perspective of a doll is used, very much as in The Tin Drum, to uncover the farcical sexual caution of the new bourgeoisie:

The doll sat under the parents' bed and heard all
When she wanted to do the same on the rocking-horse,
She said now and then again and again:
But be careful, don't you hear? be careful.

(p. 112)

And the convenient blindness and forgetfulness of conventional perception is mocked in the title of a section of the poem 'My Eraser': 'Seen through the eyes of my eraser Berlin is a beautiful town.'

The house, then, perches close to calamity, past, present, or future. But Grass's deflating wit allows no 'twilight of the gods' atmosphere to invade the poems; the images of apocalypse are appropriately absurd:[7]

The doll got a present, a ruler,
It was yellow, and so she played thunderstorms.
She broke the meter, it was just like lightning,
But thunder, the doll found that rather hard.

(p. 110)

Ausgefragt (Cross-Examined) is Grass's third substantial volume of poems (it came out in 1967). It is the most uneven of the collections, containing some first-rate work, sometimes larger and more ambitious than the earlier successes, and also some less satisfactory and questionable poems. Many of the

poems are markedly different in style from those in the previous
volumes; at the outset, they announce an aggressive departure to fresh fields and pastures new:

> Enough of similes,
> chewing the cud and splitting hairs,
> of waiting for my gall to write.

> (*Poems of Günter Grass*, p. 47)

There are gains and losses. Gone indeed are some of the more
pretentious gestures of *The Advantages of Windfowl*, the
comparings of worries to watches: the language is generally
crisper, more natural and conversational. But also gone from
some of the poems at least is the kind of taut economy that
distinguishes the best poems of *Gleisdreieck*, the capacity to
structure tightly round a single image or group of images.
Many of the political poems, of which the most famous are
those contained in the section 'ZORN ARGER WUT'
('ANGER VEXATION RAGE') are unconvincing. These
poems, attacks on fashionable protests, protestors and
protesting poets, are uncertain in their tone: at times they
engage complex and meaningful problems concerning the
worth and effectiveness of literary protest, bringing themselves (poems protesting against protests) dynamically into
the issue. At other times their sarcasm is crass and their
propositions dubious:

> There is a motion for a restraining clause:
> Never again shall we protest without power.

> (*Poems of Günter Grass*, p. 79)

This conclusion, 'no protest without power', which the author
seems to support, is the kind of unthinking slogan which
Grass's socialist critics not unreasonably dismiss (it would
gladden the heart of many a dictator). Grass's gradualist,
liberal critique of flashy revolutionaries is much better (and

---

104 GÜNTER GRASS

certainly more economically) expressed in a little four line poem in the same collection, descended from Brecht and the Imagists:

'Tour de France'

When the leading group
Was overtaken
By a brimstone butterfly,
many riders gave up the race.

(*Gesammelte Gedichte*, p. 208)

It's the touch of colour (in German 'brimstone butterflies' are 'Zitronenfalter') that gives the poem its subtle bite.

Still, the political poems are related to a concern that runs through all Grass's poems, the relation between the writer in the process of formulating his phrases, and the realities he wishes to convey. In *Advantages of Windfowl* this concern is made apparent in frequent images of the printed text itself, the shape of the type on the page: the pair of poems 'K, der Käfer' ('K, the beetle') and 'V, der Vogel' ('V, the bird') are the most obvious examples, using the shape of the letters as visual emblems of the experiences described, the one about a beetle on its back like the letter K on its side, the other developing its images out of the wedge-shaped letter V and the silhouette of birds in flight:

V, the bird, a wedge
tears open an apple, lays bare a brain,
inserts the gorges of mountains . . .

(*Gesammelte Gedichte*, p. 69)

In *Gleisdreieck* poems like 'In the Egg' ask Platonist questions about language, whether we live in a cave of language, and whether words are not about things but merely about other words:

But we have a roof over our heads.
Senile chicks,
polyglot embryos
chatter all day
and even discuss their dreams.

And what if we're not being hatched?
If this shell will never break?
If our horizon is only that
of our scribbles, and always will be?
We hope that we're being hatched.

(*Poems of Günter Grass*, p. 35)

And in *Ausgefragt* the subject of poems like 'Writing' is the poet's perhaps meaningless attempt to find the exact word to fix reality with concepts, 'to hit the inexact exactly.' (*Gesammelte Gedichte*, p. 172).

Grass thus displays his adherence to a modernist myth of language – its mistrust of the abstract written sign and its attempt to concretize words through a maximal use of their physical presence on the page. It is well known that Grass does his writing in a standing position, as if he were wielding a chisel and working at a sculpture as he had done as an art student, and that he writes the first drafts of his works in longhand; his narrative are likewise conscious of the physical act of writing (Brauxel/Amsel disapproves of Matern's habit of writing directly with a typewriter, Oskar equates black marks on white paper with guilt). It is particularly striking that each volume of poems is accompanied with drawings of the animals and objects that are so frequently the subjects of these works. These drawings have an important role in realizing the meaning of the poems, mediating the gap between the abstract signs of language and the concrete realities of experience.

At the heart of Grass's work is a mistrust of language as a deceitful structuring of reality. Harry Liebenau, the budding poet of *Dog Years*, whose penchant for pretentious metaphor and redundant statement makes him a plausible author of *The Advantages of Windfowl*, senses the frustration of trying to fit a static verbal formulation to the dynamism of experience: 'In fifth I coined the expression: "The new soloist leaps so slowly a pencil could follow." That is what I still call leaps that are skilfully delayed: leaps that a pencil could follow. If only I could follow leaps with a pencil.' (*Dog Years*, p. 247). In the novels, Grass's strategy is to unmask the inadequacy of language by inventing multiple, patently artificial verbal patterns. In some of the best of his poems he adopts an opposite strategy, concentrating on making the language as minimal as possible.

NOTES

1. *Text und Kritik* 1/1a, 18.
2. See Wieser, p. 12.
3. ibid., pp. 149–50.
4. The unattributed translations of poems in this chapter are my own.
5. This of course overlaps with the treatment of objects in the early novels.
6. See Wieser, pp. 14ff., especially for the comments on Grass's poem, 'Racine changes his coat-of-arms', in which Grass opposes the 'rat and cygne' of Racine's name.
7. All apocalypses in Grass's writing are absurd. The model for parody may be Wagner's *Götterdämmerung*. In *Dog Years* Grass structures the novel around false apocalypses: (i) Brauxel's date, Feb. 4th; (ii) Hitler's fall; (iii) the descent into Brauxel's scarecrow mine.

THE PLAYWRIGHT

Between 1954 and 1957 Grass struggled to gain recognition as a playwright, producing a series of four full-length and two one-act plays. These works, however, failed to create enthusiasm amongst West German producers or critics: one or two of them were given performances, but failed to achieve success. Somewhat later, according to Grass himself, looking back slightly sardonically on this period, he decided to give up playwriting, at least until this first batch of plays aroused some more striking response. Thereupon he set about writing *The Tin Drum*.

This decision was obviously a wise one. Since then Grass has achieved international success with his novels, and in consequence the plays have been given frequent performances; yet they have won relatively few admirers. There is wide feeling that for once the professional men of the theatre may have been right, and that Grass's plays, for all the vividness of the ideas or images they project, are lacking in dramatic vitality and energy. Marianne Kesting's criticism of *The Wicked Cooks*, that it is basically a single image inflated to the length of five acts,[1] seems applicable not only to that play but to other early plays in which the dramatic conception seems fundamentally static.

The problem emerges in Grass's first full-length play *Flood*, completed in 1955 and first performed in 1957. In this play, what happens is that nothing happens; the anticipated events turn out as 'non-events', the climaxes as anti-climaxes. The basic idea, of a house threatened by rising flood waters, a mock-parallel of the biblical flood, of itself seems to tend

towards stasis (it is reminiscent of the imagery of the poems):
little can happen except an apocalypse or a recession of the
waters. The waters simply recede. Noah's son returns home,
in parody of the prodigal son, but finds himself still in bitter
conflict with his father; at the end of the play he thinks of
murdering him, but refrains, for it would simply be a
dramatic cliché. The daughter Yetta enters a meaningless
sexual adventure with Leo's friend Congo; it leads nowhere,
and she ends the play bored and back in the arms of her more
conventional fiancé. In the final lines she longs for a real
'flood' to shatter normality more thoroughly and finally. The
play seems to be about the tedium of post-war bourgeois life,
its trivial, material values reinstated, its moral emptiness
manifest in the apparent imperviousness to the catastrophe it
manages to survive. Nothing can shock or dent the self-
complacency of the characters of *Flood*.

In its emphasis upon bathos the play shows the influence of
a whole modernist tradition in drama. From Chekhov
onwards, one of the ways in which the modernist antipathy
towards plot in a nineteenth century sense is expressed is in a
denial of the traditional significance of 'events'; they reflect
for modernist writers a false notion of time as a coherent
sequence of causes and effects. In particular it seems likely
that Grass, writing in the mid-fifties, was influenced by
Beckett's *Waiting for Godot; Flood* is not the only play of this
period structured around an anticipated event that either
fails to materialize or is a dismal bathos. Yet whereas in
Beckett's play the waiting is charged with dramatic energy
and tension, in *Flood* the representation of boredom and
inertia is in itself rather flat and boring.

Why is this? Again, there is an overlapping of themes with
Grass's novels – *Cat and Mouse* is largely about boredom,
Dog Years about the absurdity of historical and temporal
process. In the novels, these themes are conveyed through a
wealth of realist detail that creates a precise and specific time
and place as their essential context. It is noticeable that in

Flood Grass also insinuates realist details referring to a specific local context: the treatment of Betty's mania for photographs, and the reminiscences of the past that these invoke, bears resemblance in more than one respect to the parallel episodes in *The Tin Drum*. But this use of detail is very much less effective in the play than in the novel; for one thing, it has to be a good deal more compressed, and so becomes fragmentary and esoteric. When Grass uses an expressionist technique to introduce Noah's son Leo – he springs out of one of the packing cases containing Betty's photographs – there is an abrupt and awkward stylistic change from realism to stylization and 'the absurd'.

Despite Grass's confident assertion in 1961 (after the success of *The Tin Drum*) that these plays 'just like my lyrics and my prose, have in them fantastic and realistic elements that exert friction and control on each other'[2] the evidence of *Flood* points to an opposite conclusion – that Grass had not yet learnt to integrate realistic and fantastic elements, and that these conflict with each other rather than combine effectively. The telling thing is the absence of any dynamic involvement of the audience in the play, to give point to the stylistic shifts; Grass had not yet acquired the confident control of audience response that he deploys so convincingly in narrative art. Certainly it is interesting that some of the livelier moments of *Flood* are stretches of narrative; the pair of rats Pearl and Point, otherwise a mechanical device for choric comment on the moral turpitude of the human characters of the play, spring to life when Point starts to tell stories about his past, and Pearl evidently responds enthusiastically:

> PEARL ... Tell me about the convent.
> POINT You know that one already.
> PEARL Who cares? Go on. Get started.
> POINT Well, that was after my second trip to Paris. I went to a kind of lodging-house.

PEARL An old people's home, you mean?

POINT That's right. A Catholic institution in Düsseldorf on the Ratherbroich. Fine location. Right near the rail-road tracks, two steps from the junkyard, and the place itself, believe you me, it was tops. Great big cellars, nice and dark, plenty of cracks and dampness. I was rolling in clover, so to speak.

PEARL I can imagine. You always were a voluptuary. But what about the nuns?

POINT Just what you'd expect. The kitchen and living quarters were upstairs. And sometimes they came down to the cellar to get something. I'd be on the lookout and when one of them came waddling in I'd take quick aim and dart in under her habit.

PEARL You're a riot.

POINT Then I'd climb up her leg, they wear heavy woollen stockings, and I'd give her a good nip in the calf, and she'd let out a scream and drop everything.

PEARL What did she drop?

POINT Maybe a bowl. One time a dish full of peas. Full to the brim. Believe you me. Soon as the nun was gone, I made a beeline for the peas. (*Four Plays*, pp.32–3).

The vitality of interest here in such matters as the precision of specific local detail, the creation of a distinctive, rats-eye point-of-view, the exploits of a rascally itinerant hero suggests that Grass's progression from writing plays to writing novels was not fortuitous.

The Wicked Cooks seems to me a different kind of failure than *Flood*, suggesting profundities that are really much too banal to be taken seriously. It is difficult to accept Esslin's reading of the play as a modern re-enactment of Christ's crucifixion[3] or Leonard's secular variant, in which an intel-lectual aristocrat is hounded by philistine plebeians,[4] for such interpretations are alien to Grass's consistently skeptical and mocking usage of symbolic terms. What makes *The*

Wicked Cooks so indigestible is not so much the turgidity of its symbolic vocabulary as the uncertainty and redundant pomposity of its humour.

Like *Flood* the play follows a bathetic trajectory: a group of cooks attempts to worm out the secret of a mysterious recipe for a favourite soup from its creator 'Count' Herbert Schymanski, but when in the fifth act they seem on the point of success (one of them, [Vasco], having traded his girlfriend for a promise to reveal the recipe) the Count declares that he has forgotten it because of the new happiness he has found in love. A comparison with Ionesco's *The Chairs* is useful; there, an old couple play host to a phantom company assembled to hear the profundities of an eagerly awaited 'Orator', who turns out to be a deaf-mute incapable of communicating anything more illuminating than 'Angelfood'. In both cases the focus of interest is a text, an artistic message (in Grass's play the recipe is referred to as a 'poem') which promises to offer hidden truths or consolation but turns out to be hollow.

Grass's sense of form is, however, less classical than Ionesco's; whereas *The Chairs* concentrates its energies and exploits the pathos of the old couple's delusions, *The Wicked Cooks* proliferates motifs, saturating its audience with potentially significant material. Vasco parodies da Gama, and the cooks' search is a parody of the quest motif in literature; the cooks' uniforms are white, which connects them with nurses, eggs, innocence, etc; white is played against grey, the colour of the soup, made (it is said) from ashes; which in turn can be connected with images of guilt bringing us back to Vasco's uneasy conscience. And so on. The deficiency seems to be that this material is purely *verbally* generated, does not translate into effective theatre. The play is a storehouse of those trite little similes and personifying metaphors that dis-figure some of Grass's early poems, which are merely whimsical and self-conscious:

THE COUNT . . . Oh, yes, Vasco! He wanted something
from me and shook me. . . . Like a nut tree. Except that
no nuts fell out of my crown. (p. 183).

THE COUNT Your questions are stepping on each other's
heels. You're looking in the wrong spot. Not here in my
heart! On the street in a trash can – or sometimes the
wretched secret walks about. On three legs, very slowly,
like a lame dog, it limps from tree to tree, leaving a dim
shadow of its lusterless existence. (pp. 214–5).

VASCO . . . But if he don't know any longer, I ask ya! If
there was that eraser – love – and it rubbed out everything in his mind, and in his heart, and he don't know
anything any more . . . (pp. 215–6).

For English readers, the play's cause is not furthered by a
change of translators.

Again the comparison with *The Tin Drum* is irresistible.
Whereas in the novel the associative list of images derived
from the word 'white' have a purpose as ironic strategies
designed to implicate the reader in the process of perceiving
the proliferation of symbols, in the play the constant references to white become redundant. The chapter 'In the Onion
Cellar' says a great deal more about guilt in post-war
Germany than this whole play; there both the recipe and the
humour are a good deal less coy than the ash-grey soup of
The Wicked Cooks.

Though not one of Grass's more important works, the best
of these early plays is *Onkel, Onkel*. Bathos is once more a
significant structuring device: for three acts the systematic
mass-murderer Bollin fails to add to his list of victims, and
then in the fourth act himself falls prey to children who pester
him for his gun. Yet the essential difference from the other
two plays is that *Onkel, Onkel*, instead of proliferating merely
verbal motifs, generates incidents; the play is an interesting
step in the direction of the episodic structure of Grass's novels.

The acts are given titles, like chapter headings. Though the first three acts repeat each other in structure, there is variation in the presentation of the theme.

Moreover, the theme of the play comes across with relative clarity. At the beginning of Act IV Bollin thinks back on his career as a killer of opera singers, and reminds us unmistakeably of another mass-murderer with artistic pretensions:

> . . . And then my great period with Wagner. Time and again he gave me new strength. When I was half crushed by work and responsibility, when I was ready to give up, yes, give up, it was his leitmotifs that lifted me above the vexations of everyday life.

> (p. 113).

Hitler, too, adored Wagner, projected himself as wrestling (on behalf of the German people) with fearsome tasks and responsibilities, loved rhetorical repetitions and attempted to glamorize everyday life. Like Hitler, Bollin manages to win middle-class friends without much difficulty – one of the essential ironies of the play is that Bollin's intended victims are extremely accomodating towards their murderer. In Act I Sophie is bored (the theme is handled much more deftly than in *Flood*) and readily welcomes Bollin's sinister visit to her hospital ward; her mother is excited at meeting someone whose face she's seen in the papers. With obvious satiric point, neither of them is much perturbed by hints of violence or the presence of a gun; when Bollin leaves it behind at the end of the scene, Mrs Domke hands it back reassuringly: 'Anyway, you'd have found it on Sunday. Addi, my oldest boy, knows all about those things. He'd have taken good care of it.' (p. 81). Addi's 'Germanic' behaviour shows that he was well named after the Führer.

The forester in Act 2, like some less fortunate victims of Nazi cruelty, helps to dig his own grave; he manages to escape from it by deploying patriotic *Blubo* nature-mysticism, sentimentality towards children and oratorical skill, in appropriate measures. In Act III the *diva* Mimi Landella arranges for herself a perfect Wagnerian *Liebestod*, complete with photographer, to win fame for herself; unfortunately or otherwise, she kisses Bollin at a critical moment, and he, puritanically concerned not to sully his image as a 'normal' man, therefore recoils from committing the murder. This is perhaps the most successful of the episodes, and certainly satirically acute in its handling of the idea of murder as a fine art. Mimi is very much concerned about taste; she worries whether her make-up is sufficiently healthy-looking for the murder; when Bollin pulls a knife and says there'll be plenty of colour about, she reproaches him for his crudeness. Bollin, for his part, narrates with equal approval the tasteful death of the Wagnerian soprano Edeltraut Probstfeld, complete with candlelight, records of *Tristan*, and Wagnerian rhetoric on Bollin's part: '*Ruhig und wie von leiser Wehmut bewegt, hat sie gelauscht*'/' Calmly, as though stirred by gentle melancholy, she listened.' – (p. 108). Evidently the bourgeois like their violence *mild und leise*. The scene is perhaps Grass's first successful representation of the aesthetic evasion of reality that has become one of his major themes.

Onkel, Onkel, while it doesn't involve its audience directly as do the novels, nonetheless exhibits a much more interesting and confident strategy of manipulating expectations than is apparent in the other early plays. The withholding of the murders is functional; the audience finds its vicarious interest in violent action constantly thwarted. Then, in the fourth act this pattern is broken by means of a simple but effective device: murder is committed not by any monstrous hand but by ostensibly 'innocent' children. Slick and Sprat, with their perpetual begging for material goods (even secondhand ones will do, they say, appropriately for the fifties), are in fact the representatives of an acquisitive, materialistic bourgeoisie.

It is certainly ironic, then, that reviews of the first performance in Cologne in 1958 showed no sign of being able to locate the reference to reality in *Onkel, Onkel*. Even as late as June 1961, by which time *The Tin Drum* had made Grass's feelings about recent German history fairly clear, we find the reviewer of a performance in Göttingen writing: 'The "hero" of his play is derived from the line of serial murderers in Germany, from Kürten and Haarmann to Pleil.'[5] The omission of reference to more illustrious mass-murderers gives an indication of the complacent and forgetful readership that Oskar scorns in *The Tin Drum*.

In 1961 Grass took part in a discussion in Hamburg about the frustrations and difficulties of writing for the theatre in West Germany. After describing his own setbacks, he hinted at a possible return to writing plays (he was by then a successful novelist). He suggested that, having written some 'dramatic novels' he might try a different approach to the theatre: 'In short, I am writing dramatic prose and later perhaps it will work the other way round and we shall again have an epic theater.'[6]

Grass obviously had Brecht in mind and it is significant that his return to the stage, in 1966, is a play about Brecht, *The Plebeians Rehearse the Uprising*. The play challenges Brecht's classic and pre-eminent status as a dramatist in Germany: it criticizes him both as an artist and as a political example. This encounter has a ritualistic quality, for Grass by this time is offering himself as a moral and artistic example to the German public in an attempt to dethrone Brecht.

This aspect of the play is fascinating from several points of view, not least a psychological one. Nonetheless, it is not the most important question raised. Whilst the confrontation with Brecht cannot be ignored, at a more interesting level the play is concerned with the problems of the artist (Brecht and Grass included) working in a pluralist society. Its multiplicity of levels provides an adequate artistic vehicle for engaging those problems at a serious level.

The tone adopted by Grass in his speech about *Coriolanus* in 1964 (delivered to the Academy of Arts and Letters in Berlin in celebration of the Shakespeare centenary) doesn't begin to suggest this degree of significance. It is a confused performance: Grass launches into a vigorous attack on Brecht's adaptation of Shakespeare's play, with no reference to Brecht's theory or practice of rewriting classics, and makes the assumption that Brecht's *Coriolanus* can be criticized for its lack of faithfulness to Shakespeare's original. His main charges are that Brecht is consistently inaccurate and wanton in his treatment of Shakespeare's text (he is, of course, and intended to be), and that Brecht distorts the point of Shakespeare's *Coriolanus* by devaluing Coriolanus as hero and elevating the status of the plebeians and their representatives (this of course again is precisely what Brecht intended to do, on thoroughly coherent theoretical grounds). There is some wit in Grass's otherwise pedantic defence of the purity of Shakespeare's text against Brecht's tampering, but the fundamental confusion is apparent in the way Grass is quite happy to press contradictory charges against Brecht. There seems to be a good deal of wilful misunderstanding in this performance.

Brecht's *Coriolanus* is a far more interesting and important piece of contemporary theatre than Grass is willing to allow. Yet it stems from theories about the adaptation of the classics developed in the twenties, in which the stylization and simplification of the basic narrative line have a prominent place. Nothing could be further from Grass's habitual narrative practice, and I think it can be argued that the antipathy (in so far as it transcends issues of ambition and jealousy) reflects the difference between a writer who belongs to the reaction against expressionism in the twenties and a writer who belongs in the pluralist world of the sixties.

Unfortunately traces of the tone of the speech survive into the play itself. Especially in the earlier scenes, there is some slanting of the material to jeer at Brecht and his reputation.

As the play opens, a dummy of Coriolanus in spartan costume is introduced, and its relation as an image of excessive pride to 'Brecht' himself in the play is heavily underlined:

> LITTHENNER The Boss says that Coriolanus' sartorial simplicity is meant to underline his heaven-storming pride.
> PODULLA (laughing): Naturally. He's a careless dresser himself, he only changes his shirt when he has to.
> LITTHENNER (Looking at him. After a pause): You don't suppose . . . ?
> PODULLA No, I don't suppose.
>
> (*The Plebeians Rehearse the Uprising*, p. 42)

The pauses and dots are the stock-in-trade of the drama of Ibsen, as hints of repressed psychological depths; as a means of expressing veiled criticism of Brecht, they are unintentionally comic. This is before 'Brecht' has entered the play, and in case any member of the audience hasn't picked up the point that he is a proud man, Grass underlines it at the Boss's first entrance:

> BOSS Why this darkness?
> PODULLA Work lights. Same as yesterday.
> BOSS But this is a day of brightness. More light, Kowalski. In my mind and in Rome it's daylight. . . . (*Bei mir und in Rom ist es Tag*).
>
> (p. 42)

Grass gives Brecht as a first line the famous last line of Goethe ('More light'), to emphasize his pretensions as a classic writer; and as if that weren't enough, he throws in the sentence that seems to equate 'Rome' with 'my mind' to clinch his heavy-handed announcement of the character's Coriolanian *hubris*.

It is easy to conclude that the play remains at a specific level, so particularized are the references to Brecht's biography, yet the effort to perceive another level is rewarding. The details are not simply intended to attack Brecht but are also an attempt to build a different kind of epic theatre than Brecht's. It is the theatre of a realist novelist, based on the events of 17 June, 1953.

The Plebeians reads best, (and it is probably best *read*), as a link between the earlier and the later documentary novels exploring the theme of aesthetic evasion of reality; it portrays an inadequate response to the Workers Uprising in East Berlin. But by taking as its main target an artist (and not as in the Danzig trilogy the *petit bourgeois*) it raises issues that also question the adequacy of Grass's own portrayal of these historic events. For Grass's play also manifestly distorts and stylizes what happened during the Workers Uprising as much as Brecht distorts Shakespeare's *Coriolanus*. Brecht *wasn't* rehearsing *Coriolanus* on that day, and didn't write his cryptic letter supporting the regime's suppression of the Uprising on the evening of 17 June; nor, of course, did the Workers of East Berlin speak the Schillerian blank verse given to them in Grass's play. Grass's play is an aesthetic version of reality and as such suggests a much more complex reality, and a much more interesting set of problems than the confrontation with Brecht at first sight seems to raise.

In characteristic manner, Grass proliferates levels of reality in his play. This creates a hall of mirrors effect, comparable in some respects to Genet's writing, but with a much firmer relation to history. At every point the play offers ambiguities arising out of this multiplication of levels. Which plebeians are rehearsing which uprising? We have here at least four possibilities: there are the characters in Shakespeare's play, revolting against Coriolanus, the characters in Brecht's adaptation, the actors in Brecht's theatre, dissatisfied with their Coriolanus boss, and lastly the workers of East Berlin. The wealth of parallels quickly overwhelms the specific references to Brecht's biography, and the figure 'Brecht' becomes a test case rather than a specific individual. More importantly still, the author of *The Plebeians* introduces himself into the set of parallels (as he is to do increasingly in his later work). In the play 'Brecht' is adapting Shakespeare, but Grass is also drawing upon Schiller; Shakespeare's play uses Coriolanus as a mask for writing about James I and Sir Walter Raleigh, just as Grass uses him to write about Brecht; and in Grass's play, Brecht rehearses scenes from *Coriolanus* that are neither in Brecht's version nor in Shakespeare's!

The elaborate, baroque texture thus created enables the play to handle the theme of art and reality in searching ways. In important respects 'Brecht' in this play is also Grass; his very unBrechtian melancholy, as he gradually becomes aware in the play that his prediction of the failure of the uprising is correct but his actions in refusing to support it are dubious, parallels very closely the image that Grass projects of himself in *From the Diary of a Snail*. His closing line ('Bowed down with guilt, I accuse you!' – p. 112) is charged with multiple significance, referring as much to the accusations that Grass has made against Brecht as to his own. As an accuser (and it is a stance that Grass frequently adopts, particularly in his political writings), Grass frequently addresses his own participation in the guilt he condemns. *The Plebeians* is aware of itself as an aestheticization of reality, and bears a paradoxical relation to its overt intentions.

This richness of texture does not, however, make *The Plebeians* a successful *dramatic* creation for the stage. It follows the bathetic pattern of the earlier plays: it works up to the climactic point where Brecht follows a young woman, a hairdresser, to join the workers on the streets. At the point where he has, in some very qualified way, agreed to commit himself, he finds that the suppression of the uprising has begun, and the significance of his action is therefore nullified. This is a more successful use of bathos than in earlier plays, but once more banishes major action from the stage.

Moreover, many motifs in the play seem generated in verbal rather than visual terms. The stage direction as the East Berlin workers approach Brecht for his aid, is one example: '*They approach hesitantly. The* FOREMAN *compares the faces with a postcard-size picture. The lights dazzle him.*' (p. 51). A postcard size picture seems unrealizable on stage (it belongs in Oskar's album); and the 'dazzling light' is a pun, generated from 'Brecht's' desire for full lighting in Rome, standing for his Coriolanian dazzle – not something that is vividly intelligible in dramatic terms. It is also significant that the workers come asking 'Brecht' for a written statement of support, just like the cooks in *The Wicked Cooks* who are in search of a piece of paper with a recipe on it. Better propagandists then these,or more instinctive dramatists than Grass, would surely have demanded a more visually arresting symbol.

For all this, *The Plebeians* marks a much more significant stage in Grass's career than any of the earlier plays. Except in the compass of the short lyric, Grass is consistently more successful with subjects that are given by history. This play marks the turning-point from the exploitation of a past that is shaped by having been completed to the exploration of a historic present that is open-ended and incomplete.

Davor, first performed in 1969 and translated as *Uptight*, is a slighter example of what is essentially a novelist's attempt at 'epic theatre.' It is a transliteration of the novel *Local Anaesthetic*, making few concessions to the dramatic medium and attempting to prevent others from making them in its polemical stage instructions. These reflect a continuing struggle with the demon Brecht, as they ban the insertion of film or cabaret or crowd scenes. For dramatic variation, Grass reverts to the technique of his first play *Flood*, continually switching focus from one group of characters to another, each group simultaneously present on different parts of the stage. Much time is spent in discussion of events that take place before or outside the action of the play (these are handled easily in the novel as flashbacks or associations); and once more the plot proceeds towards anti-climax, as Scherbaum backs down from his plan to burn his dog on the Kurfürstendamm in Berlin. The problem posed by Scherbaum's plan, concerning the difficulty of making significant impact on the public conscience, cannot make serious headway in a play that seems to have so little interest in making popular dramatic appeal. *Davor* seems to confirm the conclusion that Grass's plays are not the most important expressions of his creative gifts.

NOTES

1. See Tank, p. 64, and Marianne Kesting, 'Günter Grass als Dramatiker', *Welt und Wort XVIII* (September, 1963), p. 270.
2. See Tank, p. 44.
3. Esslin, *The Theatre of the Absurd* (Harmondsworth: Penguin Books, 1968), pp. 260–1.
4. Leonard, p. 11.
5. See Loschütz, p. 116.
6. Tank, p. 46.

THE POLITICIAN

Grass's wholehearted commitment to political activism on behalf of the Social Democrats in Germany began with the elections of 1965. It was a controversial step; he met with opposition and mistrust, not least from members of the Social Democratic Party itself, who were often suspicious of him as a bohemian intellectual who would frighten away voters, and who in some areas dissociated themselves publicly from his initiative. He attracted large audiences, but these came for varied and often dubious reasons – to hear him read from his novels, to be scandalized by pornography or blasphemy, or as at Cloppenburg (the Worthing of West Germany) to throw rotten tomatoes. (*Günter Grass: Dokumente zur politischen Wirkung*, see pp. 36, 53).

Four years later, in the electoral campaign of 1969, Grass returned to Cloppenburg, in quite different circumstances. This time he was an officially sanctioned speaker; he was out to woo the Catholic vote, using his Cassubian background. The local Social Democrat Hans Lamp, who had disowned him in 1965, welcomed him with open arms; he was dreaming of achieving twenty-five per cent of the vote for the SPD. The chief tomato thrower of 1965 came to apologize, declaring himself a convert to left-wing radicalism (he now opposed Grass from the other side). The bohemian intellectual of 1965 had become the safe vote-catcher – perhaps the party stooge – of 1969 (see pp. 184ff).

Local Anaesthetic and *From the Diary of a Snail* cannot be properly understood or criticized without an understanding of this political activity, and the two volumes *Über das*

Selbstverständliche (parts of which have been translated as *Speak Out!*) and *Der Bürger und Seine Stimme* (*The Citizen and his Voice*), in which most of Grass's political writings are contained. The chief justification for devoting a chapter to Grass's political work is simply to provide something of that background. In addition, there is the unavoidable question of the quality of Grass's political contribution, which has, perhaps inevitably, been heavily criticized from many sides. Arguing from a position of broad acceptance of many of Grass's liberal values, I shall attempt to show that Grass has made a very distinctive contribution to West German and European political life from the specific standpoint of a practising artist.[1] This contribution has its strengths and weaknesses; it is perhaps strongest in its appreciation of the role of language, especially of ironic language, in political life, and weakest when it comes to providing a specific feasible plan of political action. Even on this point, Grass's political sense is considerably more practical and shrewd than that of, say, Solzhenitsyn.

Grass first approached politics with an obvious awareness of the mistrust that, as an artist and intellectual, he was likely to encounter. In 1965 he presents himself to the citizens of Lübeck as a liar and inventor of fictions (*Speak Out*, p. 58) – not without shrewdness in the city of Thomas Mann, where such views are relatively familiar and even respectable. Grass consistently attempts to mediate the gap between artist and politician through the use of metaphoric reassurance, revolving around oppositions of size, colour, occupation. He represents artists as members of a cosmopolitan élite ('*weltbürgerliche Elite*') who are by their nature opposed to the '*kleinbürgerlich*' (*petit bourgeois*) Social Democrats (*Speak Out*, p. 38); Grass offers his own credentials with a continual insistence on the word 'small': to go out on electoral campaigns in this manner, he says, is to go in search of 'votes, the small change of democracy.' (p. 36). The 'Revisionist's Foreword' that prefaces *Über das Selbst-*

124   GÜNTER GRASS

verständliche tells us that this book of speeches is concerned
with 'the small retail trade of democracy . . . this is no
panorama of significant world events seen from some
elevated observation-post, it was and is rather a view of the
everyday business of politics, including the very flat land of
electoral campaigns, which gave me opportunities to take
part, to get rid of some prejudices, to register little victories
or to make mistakes or revise my own standpoint.' (p. 7).
Here the imagery of size modulates into occupational
metaphor; drawing upon the background of his father's
grocery shop, Grass projects himself as a sober and respectable shopkeeper, talking frequently of 'taking stock' and
'drawing up accounts' of what progress has been achieved
towards the goals of social democracy (see for instance, *Der
Bürger und Seine Stimme*, p. 39). This rhetoric is used
conversely to denounce radicals by associating them with
bohemianism – the invasion of Czechoslavakia is not the
time for 'revolutionary theatricality' (p. 10), the 1st May is
not an occasion for an ideological 'happening' (p. 39).
Finally, Grass contrasts his own preference for shades of grey
with the garishness of extremism or idealism – social democracy is 'solid, rather colourless.' (*Speak Out*, p. 14).

With these rhetorical devices Grass attempts to win the
confidence and trust of his audience so as to broach more
theoretical issues in his political speeches. The focus of
Grass's political writings is an attack upon the German
idealist tradition in philosophy. He attempts an analysis of
its impact upon German history, and particularly upon
political extremism. Against idealism he argues in favour of
values derived from the eighteenth-century enlightenment,
and attempts to claim for social democracy a central role in
representing and furthering that tradition. He argues in
favour of the reformist view of history contained in social democracy against the revolutionary one contained in idealism.

Central to Grass's rejection of the idealist tradition is his
opposition to a Hegelian teleological view of historical

development. Grass argues that history has no goal, is not infused with any spirit of dynamic evolution; it is (as *Dog Years* shows) absurd: 'People often talk about historic missions imposed on us. I am no disciple of Hegel. I doubt whether history imposes any missions. For me, history is, to begin with at any rate, an absurd happening, into which more or less gifted people attempt to introduce some perspectives.' (*Der Bürger und Seine Stimme*, p. 110). The main thrust of Grass's objection to this tradition is based upon its psychological effects.

To take a simple example, already mentioned: Grass sees the fourteen years of Adenauer's chancellorship, between 1949 and 1963, as years in which idealism was in the ascendant. Sights were set on an ideal goal – the reunification of the whole of Germany under the political system of the Federal Republic. This ideal was an essentially unattainable one, in Grass's view; developments on the level of practical policy, such as re-armament in West Germany, the refusal to recognize or trade with the German Democratic Republic, in fact the whole of Adenauer's 'policy of strength' had in effect the opposite of the ideal political goal. Any form of reunification became more and more unlikely, the two halves of Germany polarized and grew further apart. Thus German idealism, in Grass's view, is fundamentally schizoid; the divorce of theory and practice leads to alterations of manic utopianism and depressive passivity. 'The policy of "all or nothing" has enabled us to bring in a harvest of nothing.' (*Über das Selbstverständliche*, p. 156).

The tragedy of German history, in Grass's political thinking, is the continual resurgence of idealist chimerae. As soon as the nation encounters some difficulty, like the inflation of the twenties or the depression, its nerve falters and it looks to utopian solution. The call is for the cancelling out of the past and the making of a fresh start. The lesson of the Weimar Republic is uppermost in Grass's mind and motivation. He sees the failure of artists and intellectuals to defend its institutions as partially responsible for Hitler's triumph: it is clear that this is one reason for Grass's animosity towards Brecht. He often refers to that lesson: 'It may be that I as a writer have drawn a lesson from the fall of the Weimar Republic: it wasn't only because of the National Socialist will-to-power, the opportunism of the German Nationalists, the impatience of the communists and the weakness of the democratic parties, that it broke up. The writers were involved too; the majority of them failed to stand up to protect the Weimar Republic, and not a few of them, with their wit and intelligence, deliberately made a caricature of it.' (*Der Bürger und Seine Stimme*, pp. 136–7). This, of course, helps to explain Grass's own political involvement, as a determination to ensure that the 'greyness' of social democracy shall not give way to brownness. Or some other obnoxious colour.

In his attacks upon idealism, Grass equates the extreme Left with the extreme Right – this of course infuriates socialist radicals. Rhetorically, his favourite tactic is to equate Marx and Lenin with the Pope, and Left-wing theoreticians with the scholastic philosophers of the medieval Church: Catholicism and Marxism share, according to Grass, the claim that they contain absolute truth and their teaching is therefore similiarly dogmatic. As in the case of Right-wing idealism, Grass sees in Left-wing circles a fundamental divorce between theory and praxis. Thus, in the middle and late sixties, during which the riots of 1968 took place, the Grand Coalition under Kiesinger, which united all the political parties, meant that socialists could not find any parliamentary outlet for their energies. Hence the development of a renewed utopianism, the call for a violent overthrow of the existing system and a radical new departure. This thinking, according to Grass, is quite impractical: the idea of a revolutionary alliance between students and workers is a fantasy in the heads of well-fed student theorists, who have no real concrete idea of the lives and aspirations of working-class people and whose fundamental attitude towards them is an arrogant assumption of their political backwardness.

Grass thinks that many Left-wing radicals embrace revolution as a romantic adventure: his critique of aestheticism emerges here again. The utopian content of their thinking manifests itself for Grass in a preoccupation with distant issues at remote points of the globe; he represents them rather in the manner of Dickens's portrait of Mrs Jellyby in *Bleak House*, concerned about doing good for the natives of Borrioboola-Gha while entirely neglecting her own family. This message comes across strongly in his writings on the 'Prague Spring' of 1968, and the failure of the German radical Left to concern themselves adequately with an issue next door to them '. . . . the students of Berlin and Paris did not take Vaculik or Havel as their model; their choice was photogenic and aesthetic: Che Guevara, the Argentine professional revolutionary, was enlarged to pin-up size. In other words: while the Czechoslavakian reformers were trying to put through their reform under the most discouraging conditions and to overcome obstacles which, as we have recently seen, are still insuperable, the Western radical Left – also termed the New Left – indulged in romantic revolutionary gestures.' (*Speak Out*, p. 137). The familiar imagery of the house is dominant in Grass's thinking here: those who revere 'freedom fighters' often see the struggle as an escape from the narrow and restricting boundaries of the home and familial responsibility. Grass reflects bitterly on the German romantic idealization of departure into battle, and into death: 'Thousands of postcards from the year 1914 show the German or French *pater familias* tearing himself away from his wife and kids (that is to say, the burden of family, office hours, rules and regulations) and looking squarely at the free death of a free man (that is to say, the death of a soldier).' (p. 27).

Lastly, Grass is scornful of what he sees as the ineffectuality of protests and demonstrations. These are reactions against events that have taken place already; worse still, the causes about which protests are made are quickly forgotten, as new issues emerge to take their place. On this last point Grass is often impressive; he understands acutely the ephemerality principle built into the news media, and he sees the radical Left taken in and fragmented by a series of competing disasters. It is not surprising that this should be a major theme of Grass's political thinking, for it links closely with his purpose as an artist to keep the past alive: 'remember Czechoslovakia' has distinctive meaning for Grass.

It is now necessary to turn to Grass's theoretical defence of social democracy. He acknowledges as intellectual mentor the nineteenth century theoretician Eduard Bernstein, who at the SPD party congress at Erfurt in 1891 led the reformist section of the party, those that rejected revolutionary paths to socialism and put forward a programme of reform, to be achieved through parliamentary means, that would lead by a gradual evolutionary process towards fulfilment of socialist aims. It was from this congress that the split between Marxists and Social Democrats on the German Left began to develop, and Bernstein, who had been a friend and close collaborator of Engels in exile in England, was branded as a revisionist. In his political writings Grass takes upon himself the title of revisionist to express his adherence to Bernstein and his view of the proper notion of historical development.

In this view, there is no sequential linear development from capitalism to socialism: those countries that have experienced revolution in the name of socialism have merely discovered that capitalism turns up in another form, that of state capitalism. Capitalism and socialism exist side by side; 'they influence and condition each other . . .' (*Der Bürger und Seine Stimme*, p. 78). History is a process of continual reform: revolution is at best a wasteful digression. Eberhard Starusch's teaching in *Local Anaesthetic* conveniently gathers the scattered statements on revolution to be found in Grass's political writings:

Finally I demonstrated how – and how insatiably – the Revolution devours its children. (Büchner's Danton as a witness to absurdity.) And it all ended in reformism. With a little patience, they could have had the same thing at less cost. That's where Napoleon came in. Revolution as repetition. Short excursions: Cromwell, Stalin. Inevitable absurdities: revolution creates restoration, which has to be eliminated by revolution.

(*Local Anaesthetic*, p. 131).

Even reform itself cannot be seen as an ideal, according to Grass, for there is a kind of dialectic operating within the process of reform. Each act of social progression brings with it as a consequence the need for further reform, to balance out or to make it properly effective: 'To put it in a complex way: changes become possible because of changes and release changes, which again make possible further changes. So every reform that looks at itself in isolation, will fail from a lack of insight into its own consequences.' (*Der Bürger und Seine Stimme*, p. 86). Every act of reform is, therefore, strictly relative, part of a process, never something that can be abstracted and hailed as an abolute – this in Grass's terms would be anti-historical. So for instance the need for reform of education, which is one of Grass's most frequent and fervent concerns, is no more an end in itself than any other goal:

I don't expect a solution from a new type of school for I don't believe in any absolute solution, only in a further step in the process of evolution. Nor do I think that there is such a thing as justice. There can only be favourable circumstances in which there is more justice, a good proximation of it. We shall have to learn that there are circumstances in which a step towards greater justice carries with it new injustices, which then have to be ironed out again. (p. 113).

Grass is fond of reiterating as Social Democratic principles the values of the European enlightenment: rationality, moderation, freedom of individual conscience, tolerance. Tolerance in particular is seen by Grass as a cornerstone of his revisionist philosophy: one of his favourite slogans is from Rosa Luxemburg (claimed by Grass as a revisionist), 'freedom always means the freedom of the person who thinks otherwise than oneself.' It is part of the protocol of Grass's political involvement that the Christian Democrats are always to be described as opponents and never as enemies (the piece on the death of Adenauer is entitled 'Obituary of an Opponent'). And in addressing a congress of writers in Yugoslavia he insists on respecting ideas with which he does not agree; this is because 'literature demands realities – for there are several. Yours, a Yugoslavian one, I should like to find out more about; and I am glad to give reports of my German one. I start from the premise that your reality and mine must not exclude each other.' (p. 72).

This is one of a number of statements in which Grass commits himself unequivocally to living in a pluralist society. The progressive Social Democrats accept as part of the necessary richness of society a multiplicity of viewpoints and interests; in order to achieve any kind of reform, these must be taken into account. 'Compromise' is a frequent and positive word in Grass's political writings, involving the recognition of plural realities. And 'contradictions' are not part of the superstructure of capitalist society in a decadent phase, but rather the essential features of human societies, to be tolerated and celebrated (see p. 169).

All Grass's political activity has a strongly pedagogic flavour. He sees himself as an educator helping to nurture parliamentary democracy in Germany. His language is full of educational and developmental imagery; opponents who will not accept the 'lessons' of history are branded as 'immature', the goal is to achieve a mature democratic society which is able to acknowledge responsibility for the consequences of its actions (the theme of the novels are evident here). And in his contributions to the topic of educational reform, Grass shows himself advancing the same pluralist values as elsewhere: what he values is comprehensive education, the development of interdisciplinary curricula, the simultaneous study of multiple inter-related phenomena.

What are the deficiencies of Grass's political opinions? Grass, as has frequently been pointed out, is the not unfamiliar type of 'fanatical moderate' who, in proselytizing for tolerance often reveals himself as surprisingly intolerant. There are some very irritating passages in Grass's political writings, where rationalized prejudice predominates over enlightenment rationality. These are particularly frequent when Grass denounces fellow writers for their political views (he lumps together the most heterogenous figures, such as Brecht and Heidegger, Ilya Ehrenburg and Ezra Pound, as on p. 70) or where he jeers at middle-class students. In the latter case, the sense of an unexamined resentment at having been educationally deprived because of war is irresistible.

Moreover, many of Grass's political judgments are patently faulty. Manfred Jäger[2] is one of many who have observed that Grass, despite his invectives against idealism, is very fond of designing utopias. His are of a pluralist and liberal variety. On one occasion, for instance, Grass proposes the reintegration of Germany within a federal framework (see Über das Selbstverständliche (p. 160)). He seems to have the model of Italy in mind, with some provinces communist, others conservative; Grass, an admirer of the Italian communist party, appears not to perceive its fundamental difference from that of the German Democratic Republic. Nor does he seem to take into account the fact that provinces have no political status within the GDR.

Whenever fantasy appears in Grass's political thinking, one senses that Danzig is in some way connected. This is certainly the case with a superficially appealing idea that Grass puts

forward in a speech called 'What is the German Fatherland?'
(pp. 32ff.). He urges the foundation of new cities within the
German Federal Republic, with names like 'New Breslau'
and 'New Danzig'. Then all the displaced people from the
'lost provinces' can get together, resurrect their old dialects,
carry on their old customs, give up joining the neo-Nazi
party, and recognize the boundaries of Poland because they
won't want to hanker after old Danzig or Breslau any more.
An equally fanciful idea solves the problem of immigrant
workers in Germany at a stroke: Grass climbs the hill of
Kreuzberg in Berlin (a working-class suburb heavily popu-
lated with Turks) and sees a vision of a federal Berlin, made
up of quarters and suburbs for each nationality, with a
minaret for the Turks, a campanile for the Italians, etc. (see
Der Bürger und Seine Stimme, pp. 210–2).

Yet even these flights of fancy are not wholly devoid of
humour. Irony is an essential feature of Grass's political
attitudes: it is a means of creating a detachment which can
make possible the contemplation and understanding of
contemporary life. In *Dog Years* irony is an essential
component of the liberalism of Eddi Amsel, and in the
political writings it is used as a kind of barometer of rationality. In Grass's view, the extreme Left and extreme Right are
also united in their absence of humour, and this lack is itself
part of the tragedy of German history. A passage about the
discussion of educational reform makes this clear:

> . . . I suggest that the discussion of educational reform
> might be carried out less bitterly, and without that deadly
> Germanic seriousness which has always furnished our
> schools and made them look like funeral parlours. You
> only have to listen and look around. You find the
> question of the curriculum stylized away into the
> question of destiny. You find conservative pathos
> confronting progressive pathos. You find all over the
> country that irony – health-giving, because it creates

distance – is excommunicated as a symptom of decadence. (p. 189).

The idea of the meaning and purpose of distance in another dimension crops up in the context of a discussion of the tempo of contemporary life. For Grass it is the speed with which events succeed each other that prevents us from achieving an understanding of our condition; art can be the means of creating the distance necessary to provide that perspective: 'When are the pauses reached? What kind of works of art are necessary to gain distance – even for the length of a hyphen?' (p. 189).

Finally, we come to perhaps the most important feature of all in Grass's political writings: the vigilance about political language. It is not always apparent. There are many occasions where Grass wields political slogans in a thoroughly professional, even cynical way. But he is intensely conscious of cliché, both in politics and in other fields. In a passage about environmental politics, for instance, Grass seizes on phrases like 'protecting property' and wrings their neck: 'If you can succeed in making clear to individual citizens that their property has already been destroyed, the water they drink, the seaside where they spend their holidays, the Rhine, which is a stinking sewer despite the beautiful songs dished up about it, then you'll be able to explain to them too that this threatened property has got to be protected . . .' (p. 104). Grass has an acute ear for hangovers of Nazi terminology: when Erhard attacked 'degenerate art' in the Federal Republic, Grass was ready with his own brand of degenerate sarcasm and irreverence in reply:

He who always says 'I' has called art 'degenerate', he, the Elected One, has invoked that monstrosity, 'healthy popular feeling', he who has once again been confirmed in office has given new life to words from Goebbels's thesaurus. Response: lamentations and helpless protests.

> Snivelling and whining as though the well-known
> philistine disguised as Chancellor hadn't shown his
> thousand-year teeth before. Old-maidish indignation in
> the editorial of the weekly *Die Zeit*, as if the butcher boy
> had farted in a convent. (*Speak Out*, p. 44).

The passage is a good example of Grass's political humour,
impaling Erhard on his own coarseness and gluttony.

For Grass, idealism and jargon are essentially linked. The
scrutiny of contemporary political rhetoric is a scanning for
signs of a resurgence of idealism. Grass diagnoses flatulence
in the rhetoric of the idealist Left: 'Already there is a confusion of language: students try to enlighten the workers and
are occasionally threatened because they speak a jargon that
no worker can understand.' (p. 117). Even within his own
party, in the case of reforms that he strongly supports, he
finds evidence of obscurantism:

> It would be a good idea to wean educational politicians
> away from a vice which – sticking to the topic – has
> formed a school of adherents: that they might at last say
> goodbye to their incomprehensible jargon of educational
> reform, so that the specialized vocabulary of a few
> reformers doesn't suddenly become the jargon of an
> élite. . . . No excuse is valid, mutterings about the pressure
> of time can't mitigate the offence. Because if progress can
> no longer articulate itself properly, it will grind to a halt
> and allow reaction to triumph.
>
> (*Der Bürger und Seine Stimme*, p. 133).

And on many occasions Grass has argued that the turgid
style of the Trade Union Press offers no competition to the
Bild-Zeitung as reading matter for working people. Crisp and
clear language is for Grass an essential condition of a vigorous
reforming democracy.

Grass abhors the word 'humanism'. It is associated in his

mind with the old-fashioned and discredited 'humanist grammar-schools' that supported authoritarianism: in *Dog Years* he describes the playground of the Conradinium as 'melancholy, Prussian, humanistic.' (p. 103). Yet the conception of an essential link between the vitality and clarity of a language and the vitality of the society that uses it is one of the main legacies of the humanist tradition in which Grass belongs. His main significance for our time may be that he sees, more clearly than most, the superior durability and truthfulness of black marks on white surfaces to ephemeral images projected on a grey screen. That, at any rate, is the subject of *Local Anaesthetic* and *From the Diary of a Snail*.

NOTES

1. This is the view also of Gertrude Cepl-Kaufmann (op. cit., p. 66). Her book is acutely penetrating about Grass's political attitudes; its defect, in my view, is its failure to allow for irony, most particularly in Grass's novels.
2. See *Text und Kritik 1/1a*, pp. 74ff.

THE CONTEMPORARY POLITICAL NOVELS

Local Anaesthetic and *From the Diary of a Snail*

As I have suggested, Grass's political writings provide a more or less indispensable basis for the understanding of his most recent writings. *Local Anaesthetic* works out in particular an attack upon linguistic confusion as it appears to Grass in the slogans of the radical Left. It embodies Grass's belief that contradictions are an essential reality of human experience, and it attempts to counter revolutionary theory through the use of a language that embraces contradiction, most obviously in the form of paradox and oxymoron. *From the Diary of a Snail* likewise attempts to enact the values that it upholds in its verbal texture: it is not simply 'about' gradualism, its structure denies teleology by conducting several narrative strands simultaneously. It also develops in a significant way the theme of the ephemerality of modern society which makes historic events become news items to be consumed and disposed of instantaneously.

Neither book has contributed a great deal to Grass's critical standing. They remain too close to the events that inspired them: partisanship figures largely in assessments of their importance. Both of them – in particular *Local Anaesthetic* – will grow in stature when the specific controversies they have excited become less acute.

Six years after the completion of the Danzig trilogy, in 1969, Grass published a new novel set in Berlin, *Local Anaesthetic*. It is fundamentally different from the earlier group of prose works in several important respects, amongst them

136

the relative insignificance of the Danzig background and the relative significance of contemporary political events, and the very different nature of the major protagonists. There is no extraordinary, quasi-mythical figure amongst the characters of *Local Anaesthetic*, to compare with Oskar or Eddi Amsel; the narrator and hero is rather a Pilenz than a Mahlke. Eberhard Starusch, forty-year-old history teacher, timid, anxiously reflective rather than active, heroic only in his fantasies, narrates most of the novel in a dentist's chair; here he confides to the dentist 'secrets' about his past and present, and in particular the personal dilemma caused by one of his favourite pupils, who threatens to burn his dog in front of a smart West Berlin café. The dentist is perhaps a descendant of Eddi Amsel, via 'The Boss' in *The Plebeians Rehearse the Uprising*, for he certainly dominates the conversation with superior insight and understanding; yet even he is no more than a prosaic, skeptical, liberal-minded professional who is the target of counter-criticism within the novel.

This move away from the Danzig material represents an important, if hazardous step in Grass's career as a writer. In several respects it parallels the move into active politics, which also seems to have signified for Grass the exchange of the vivid imaginative material of the past for the greyness of everyday reality. Certainly it accounts for some of the hostile reception of *Local Anaesthetic*; it is very difficult at first to adjust to the absence of the sensational events and eccentric characters that inhabit the earlier novel. The adjustment once made, however, *Local Anaesthetic* begins to seem more and more impressive, perhaps more thoughtful about private experience than the earlier novels, and certainly, as Angus Wilson puts it in *The Observer* of 12 May 1974, 'insufficiently recognized.'

The title *örtlich betäubt* is a succinct formulation of some of the novel's principal themes. '*Örtlich*' (local) refers not only to dental anaesthetics but also to politics, implying the immediate and near-at-hand rather than the abstract and remote in time and space. *'Betäubt'* has a similar double meaning, referring both to Novocain and to a particular issue of political theory very much alive during the student riots of 1967–8 to which the novel refers. Grass is alluding to Marcuse's analysis of the impact of advanced technology on capitalism.[1] In Marcuse's thinking, advanced capitalist societies pursue a sophisticated policy of suppressing criticism by permitting it, and stifling effective challenge by the 'anaesthetizing' of the working-class through the provision of material wealth in superfluity. Certainly Rudi Dutschke in 1968 used the concept *'Betäubung'* to describe the hypocritically masked violence of capitalist oppression: *'Liberal und rechtsstaatlich sind die Herrschenden nur, solange sie die "Abhängigen" damit betäuben können. Leisten die Abhängigen Widerstand, dann kommt der Polizeiknüppel.'* (*Günter Grass: Dokumente zur politischen Wirkung*, p. 103) ('The ruling classes are only liberal and constitutional for as long as they can *anaesthetize* their 'dependents' thereby. As soon as the dependents manage to resist, out comes the police truncheon.') my emphasis.

The logic of such arguments is that the violent nature of capitalism must be unmasked through acts of provocation. The purpose of Grass's novel is to attempt a rebuttal of this logic, and the habits of thought and language that characterize it. The ambiguity of the title is, therefore, emblematic of the view of experience that the novel upholds against abstract analyses: nothing is simple and unambiguous in reality, everything is multiple and complex. Nothing is simply good or bad; the novel offers a searching and vivid criticism of the greedy materialism of contemporary West Germany, but casts doubt on the Marcusian formula that material advances are simply 'anaesthetics'. Like Grass's political writings, the novel offers not the black-and-white of revolutionary thesis and reactionary antithesis, but rather the 'grey' of an independent critical questioning of the ills and virtues of contemporary capitalism.

Appropriately, then, the blank TV screen at which Eberhard Starusch gazes in the dentist's chair is of a neutral shade of grey. Television provides the focus for Grass's examination of Marcuse's thesis: it is clearly a primary contemporary 'anaesthetic' offering distraction from anxiety, or as here simple physical pain. Irmgard Seifert recommends the 'Doc' to Eberhard Starusch because his surgery has a television set for patients; it is ironic that such a fierce opponent of the prevailing socio-economic system as she should feel so dependent on its benefits. Not content with simple anaesthetics to suppress pain, the pampered beneficiaries of the 'Doc's' services also demand something to keep their minds off the Novocain injection: 'But to take your mind off the nasty little pinprick, I can call on our television for help . . .' (*Local Anaesthetic*, p. 62). There they watch further 'anaesthetics' in the Marcusian sense – advertisements of the miracle of capitalist technology; Grass focuses with particularly effective irony on an advertisement for deep-freezers, which parodies the 'freezing' effects of Novocain and at the same time appeals to comfortable fantasies of gluttonous food, 'snap beans, veal kidneys, and California strawberries . . . red perch fillets and iron-rich spinach.' (p. 26). The freezer advertisement leads straight back to the dentist's chair, in apparent endorsement of Marcuse's analysis of capitalist technology as a circular and self-validating species of propaganda.

Equally importantly the television set facilitates other 'anaesthetic' fantasies within Eberhard Starusch's mind. As he stares at the screen, he elaborates to the doctor the image that he sees played out upon it, concerning his past as an engineer in a large cement works during the fifties, his engagement to the boss's daughter, the breaking-up of the engagement and his fresh start as a teacher with money from his fiancée. This story is presented in a fundamentally ambiguous way; the boundaries of reality and fiction are almost impossible to chart. But at one level it is certainly a consoling myth, designed to compensate for a sense of failure by means of a dramatic heightening of the experience in question.

The ironic plot thickens when it becomes apparent that this myth of the past corresponds to radical scenarios of revolution. The idea of a violent apocalypse (Eberhard Starusch imagines himself murdering his fiancée, in several different manners) as the cleansing prerequisite for a complete reinvigoration of society is common both to Eberhard Starusch's thinking and to the ideas of Marcusian radicals: 'If I was to change, then radically. So she wouldn't have thrown away her money for nothing.' (p. 15). According to the fashionable theorists, one cannot know what the revolution is *for*, because the oppressive nature of capitalist society is such that one cannot think outside its terms: therefore, one must destroy first and think what to do afterwards. The contemplation of such possibilities provides a vicarious satisfaction for the gnawing sense of failure felt by the middle-class, middle-aged spectators of revolution, like Irmgard Seifert: 'This new generation, free from the burden of guilt – believe me, Eberhard – will put an end to the moth-eaten nightmare. These boys and girls want to start afresh; they refuse to go on squinting backwards and lagging behind their potentialities like us.' (p. 117).

The dentist perceives the motives of Eberhard Starusch's violent fantasies; half humorously, he exercises the absolute power he wields over his patients in the chair – the power of shutting off speech by going to work on the teeth: ' "I will not tolerate incitements to violence, even if put in the mouth of a former fiancée or of a minor girl student. . . . just because your fiancée has run out on you, just because you're a failure, a washout, who draws on insane fictions to show that the whole world is a failure and justify him in destroying it." ' (p. 95). The ironies are multiple: Starusch, whilst he fantasizes about violent destruction, is helplessly passive under the dentist's power; the apparently bitter opponent of fascism and state violence adopts the same kind of thinking himself, even to the extent of unconsciously parodying Hitler (who likewise concocted a fantasy of violent revenge for the sense of personal failure as a rejected art-student/soldier); and so on. The outlines of the novel's counter-attack on revolutionary thinking begin to emerge.

One of the prime tactics of this attack is the critical scrutiny of revolutionary language. It is done from a rigorous literalness of approach to language that perpetually uncovers metaphoric habits of thought in revolutionary minds. Starusch for instance, fantasizes about burning department stores – only to awake to the realization of the fact that his mind is at two metaphorical removes from the cause of these fantasies: 'Brigades on brigades of bulldozers flattened shopping centres, warehouses, spare parts depots, cold-storage plants filled with sweating mountains of butter, conglomerate production areas, intensely humming research laboratories, flattened, I say, assembly lines and conveyor belts. Department stores fell to their knees and set each other on fire. And over it all a chant: Burn, warehouses, burn – and the voice of my dentist who was trying to make me believe that he had removed the aluminium shells, that there had been a little accident, that his red-hot tweezers had branded me.' (pp. 104–5). The burnt gums produce associative metaphors built on the word 'burning' (and Starusch's whole vision recapitulates the conditions of the dentist's surgery – 'cold-storage plants', 'intensely humming research laboratories', etc.), and the warehouses stem from the slogan chanted by protesting radical students, 'burn, warehouse, burn . . .' Significantly, that chant is based upon inaccuracy; the students confuse the English word 'warehouse' with the German '*Warenhaus*' ('department store'). The inaccuracy emphasizes the looseness of revolutionary jargon, and the appeal to irrationality signified by the ritualistic chanting of the slogan is contrasted with the calm, rational voice of the dentist, bringing Starusch back to earth. The clear emphasis is that subjective associations and not an impersonal logic stir thoughts of revolution in the mind of Eberhard Starusch.

Irmgard Seifert, nicknamed 'archangel' by her students, has her own distinctive taste for metaphoric heightening, characterized by what Starusch places as a 'Late Expressionist' line in rhetorical adjectives; at the age of seventeen it had been a question of her 'blond hatred' for Bolshevism, international jewry, etc. and now it is her fervent longing for the 'yoke-breaking victory of socialism.' (p. 51). She is a casualty of the German idealist tradition, her enthusiasms again far removed from coherent argument, her flamboyant rhetoric compensating like Starusch's fantasies for personal frustrations and disappointment. Her 'lasting influence' on Vero Lewand is an ironic demonstration of the continuity of Right-wing and Left-wing radicalism, though her violent language looks like innocuous sabre-rattling compared with Vero Lewand's terse and aggressive deployment of Marcusian metaphor to prevent Starusch from arguing with Philipp Scherbaum: 'We demand: Stop tranquillizing him!' (p. 185).

This quasi-medical terminology (variations upon 'anaesthetics', 'tranquillisers' and 'pacifiers' recur frequently) is the essential focus of the novel's attack upon the way in which metaphor falsifies. Starusch begins to talk of the 'painful' things he had to face after Linde's decision to break off the engagement, and the dentist interrupts him swiftly: 'I wouldn't use the word "pain" so lightly if I were you.' (p. 60). Constantly the loose theory of the 'anaesthetics' of capitalism is confronted with the literal-minded assertion that pain is a real and inescapable fact of individual experience, that anaesthetics are the slowly and gradually evolved product of a historical development, and that their use in alleviating pain cannot but be seen as beneficial from a rational perspective. 'All people are sick, have been sick, get sick, and die' (p. 74) is the almost platitudinous premise from which the dentist's idea of a reformed system of medical welfare departs, and the novel endorses him in its concluding sentence: ('There will always be pain.' – p. 231). For Grass, theory founders on the objective and unanswerable realities of individual experience, just as its language founders on the test of its faithfulness to that experience: 'anaesthetics' cannot be evil instruments of oppression if pain is inevitable.

The conception of Philipp Scherbaum in the novel is the most important example of this testing of theory against experimental reality. I am unable to share Irène Leonard's view, that 'the fact that Scherbaum's conversion remains unexplained is the most serious fault of the novel'[2]. It seems to me that there is ample indication of the grounds for Scherbaums' change of heart, and that any further elaboration of this thinking at the time of the decision would be inartistic (equally, Grass doesn't need to belabour us with details of Starusch's sexual encounter with Vero Lewand). Scherbaum's conversion is surely brought about by an increased awareness of the contradictions which the burning of his dog must result in.

At the beginning of the novel Scherbaum is shown as a rigorous theoretician who abhors contradictions, refusing to edit the school newspaper because 'You can't reform absurdity. Or do you by any chance believe in reformed absurdity?' (p. 8). His language is implicitly contrasted with that of Starusch, whose moderation of outlook is expressed through his choice of heavily qualifying adjectives ('mild laughter' . . . 'moderate impudences' . . . 'middlingly amusing nonsense' – (p. 7) that push in the direction of oxymoron. At one level the difference is between theoretical purism and a pragmatism aware of the necessity of compromise: Scherbaum can only be 'pure' because his ideas haven't been tested against actuality (compare the discussions between Starusch and the dentist about the impossibility of purity, pp. 132–3 and elsewhere). As soon as Scherbaum commits himself to a specific course of action, the burning of his dog, he discovers complex consequences with which he had not fully bargained. The act itself requires quasi-paradoxical justification: 'I call it enlightenment by demonstration (*demonstrative Aufklärung*)' (p. 114) – a strange version of eighteenth century ideals. The decision to inform Starusch produces the most strenuous attempts to dissuade him (not on idealistic grounds!) from his course of action, Starusch even offering to do the deed himself instead. Philipp Scherbaum responds with some sensitivity both to Starusch and to the dentist; this is expressed in his adoption of Starusch's habit of oxymoron: 'The man goes to a lot of trouble to swindle honestly – like you.' (p. 160) The formulation closely echoes Starusch's immediately preceding series of paradoxical reflections about the 'Doc': 'Reactionary modernist. Solicitous tyrant. Gentle sadist . . .' (p. 160), etc. The novel depicts stages in Scherbaum's developing awareness of inherent contradictions in himself and others about him, a process which reaches its climax in his request to the dentist to anaesthetize his dog. Thereafter the decision to scrap the plan and to jettison Vero Lewand are consequential developments that require only sketching in to the novel.

The sympathetic portrayal of Philipp Scherbaum is one of the most impressive features of *Local Anaesthetic*, convincingly embodying the flexible liberal values for which the novel argues. Scherbaum is set apart from the fashionable radicals as an independent critical consciousness aware of the ironies of radical chic posturing: 'Not only myself, Scherbaum too stood there estranged. It would be unfair to mention the stale air, the noise, the motionless acrid-smelling heat, or externals such as the extravagant uniformity of dress, the hairdos, the frantic effort to be colourfully different, which cancelled others out and culminated in monotony.' (p. 164). He is an ironist, his humour attuned to the paradoxes and incongruities of relationships between apparent opposites, bourgeois and radical, aesthete and Maoist, as in his humorously distanced perception of Vero Lewand: 'He says: "Sometimes of course it's more than I can take! she reads Mao like my mother reads Rilke." ' He speaks of the sombre Che as 'Vero's pin-up.' A memory rises up in him from the grey dawn of history: 'Bob Dylan used to hang there. A present from me. "He's so damn real," I wrote in it. Oh well, that was long ago.' (p. 180). It is, therefore, appropriate that his 'conversion' should be expressed ironically: 'He says he wouldn't want to be like you, peddling the feats of a seventeen-year-old when he's forty, because, so he says, that's what you do.' (p. 198). This unsentimental statement of indebtedness to Eberhard Starusch also conveys a fully developed sense of the absurdity of history and the apparent paradoxicality of thinking about progress. 'Accelerated immobility' is what the 'Doc' calls it (p. 76).

This obviously important oxymoron suggests how central the 'Doc's' consciousness is in the novel. He is the most articulate and confident of the voices of liberal pragmatism. Yet, despite its evident thesis, the novel is far from being a simple piece of propaganda on behalf of liberal values; the dentist's position is criticized and placed in perspective by other points of view within the novel. Starusch, for instance, perceives the element of establishment complacency in the 'Doc': 'My dentist is married, has three children, is in the prime of life and practises a profession that brings gaugeable results' (p. 157), a sentence that has an even stronger sing-song banality in German. There is irony in the doctor's liberal tolerance towards fat ladies who eat cakes in the fashionable and expensive cafés of the Ku-damm; they are good for business, bringing 'gaugeable results' in the form of well-filled appointment-books. It is indicative of the flexibility of the novel that on this point Starusch takes Vero Lewand (predominantly presented in a sharply satiric manner) far more seriously than the doctor, for her tersely formulated perception of the contradictory ludicrousness of the ladies: 'Vero Lewand's estimate had been correct: "At least three pounds of jewellery apiece. And what do they talk about when they talk? Phew, about weight and dieting. Ugh!" ' (p. 153). Starusch goes on to take sharper issue with the doctor: 'Later I noted: The modesty of specialists when they speak of their difficulties and limited achievements in the arrogance of our times. This back-slapping: Yes yes, of course, we're all workers in the Lord's vineyard. . . . Their constant insistence that we must differentiate at all times, even in our dreams. Their ability to relativize even the greatest horrors . . .' (p. 159). This is an acute perception of the relativity of relativity, the awareness that the doctor's position is only a point in a continuing process, limited and shaped by the material circumstances of the society in which he works. On this front Starusch's understanding of the need for reform is superior to the doctor's; in order to supersede this level of specialist understanding, it is necessary to reform the educational system in the direction of interdisciplinary study, though here again the heavy jargon of the theorists of reform shows how far from completeness the process is: 'I mockingly quoted my colleague Enderwitz whose opinion I actually share: "The integrated pluridisciplinary school is the best possible means of facing up to the present socio-political situation.".' (p. 170). Obviously, nothing is perfect.

Nonetheless, the doctor is able to articulate most of the philosophical issues on which the novel reflects. He sees the essential reality of pain as it exists closely intermingled with consciousness itself, leaving evidence of its material sub-stantiveness in the tooth-decay that is formed through the saliva as the mind ceaselessly ruminates: 'Your tartar is your calcified hate. Not only the microflora in your oral cavity, but also your muddled thoughts, your obstinate squinting back-ward, the way you regress when you mean to progress, in other words, the tendency of your diseased gums to form germ-catching pockets, all that – the sum of dental picture and psyche – betrays you . . .' (p. 28). It is this materialist understanding of the nature of consciousness that enables the dentist to reject the traditional idealist separation of thought and action: ' "Too much action, too many one-eyed victories. Grabbing at the moon when there's still no effective tooth-

paste. Too many men of action, too many knot-cutters." . . .'
What about my dentist's assault on my prognathism which
he called congenital and therefore authentic? Wasn't that
action? He will say: Knowledge plus skill, whereas the
precipitate extraction of teeth, the mania for creating gaps
that no longer hurt, is action without knowledge: active
stupidity.' (p. 126). This line of thought of course strengthens
the argument against the idealism of the Marcusian revolutionaries, for whom one violent act of overthrow – absurd in
itself and divorced from any carefully calculated set of
consequences – is regarded as the only prospect of human
liberation. In turn, too, it has consequences for the novel's
view of the revolutionary hero; Scherbaum is entirely unlike
the glamorized guerrilla leaders of fashionable radicalism:
'No. He's not like that. Not a hero. Not interested in leading
or in gaining supporters. He can't put on that fanatical look.
He's not even impolite.' (p. 175). Each of the characters of the
novel is unheroic, limited, and mediocre, but the novel
contemplates their preoccupations seriously.

In the light of this sceptical pluralist conception of reality
the case against the followers of Marcuse is brought home. It
is the arrogance of revolutionaries that offends Grass most,
that unfounded conviction that whereas other forms of
consciousness are simply imprisoned reflections of the superstructure of economic power, revolutionary consciousness is
an absolute value. The logic is false and self-contradictory,
Grass declares; the assumption of a gulf between the analyst
of society and the society in which he lives is an idealist and
not a materialist mode of thought. The apologist for liberalism cannot rebut his opponents with the same absolute
conviction; it is in the nature of the case he attempts to make
that it has no final or exclusive hold upon truth. The novel is
constantly aware of the limitations, and the appearance of
weakness, that beset the values of tolerance. Nevertheless, it
attempts to show that there is no logically or morally
acceptable alternative.

From the Diary of a Snail continues the exploration of contemporary society begun in *Local Anaesthetic;* it appeared in Germany in 1972 and in English translation in 1973. To borrow from Huckleberry Finn's appropriately culinary language, it is a kind of barrel of odds and ends, in which things are mixed up and juices swap around, an interdisciplinary work (cognate with Grass's propaganda for interdisciplinary education) in which various kinds of writing – passages of verse, dialogue, narrative, diary-jottings, political commentary, etc. – jostle and intertwine. Grass himself refers to the book in its pages as a 'scrap-book' of part of 1969, from the election of Gustav Heinemann as President of the Federal Republic in March to the narrow victory of Willy Brandt at the polls in late September. It records Grass's own political activities during that period, the thoughts that preoccupied him and the reasons he attempted to give his family to explain his constant absence from home.

It is thus very difficult to assign the *Diary* to any single pre-existent *genre*; nevertheless, it seems important to establish first that it is an imaginative work rather than a piece of documentary autobiography. The diary or journal form is a common mode of twentieth century fiction, from Gide's *Les Faux Monnayeurs* to Sartre's *La Nausée:* it signifies the abandonment of traditional plot-structure in favour of a more faithful representation of the tangled inconclusiveness of actual experience. In addition, Grass seems to be influenced in this book by the documentary tendencies in many contemporary writings, like the plays of Rolf\Hochhuth or Truman Capote's *In Cold Blood.* The major point to emphasize, however, is that its multiplicity of form is a polemical expression of Grass's pluralist thinking about art as well as political life.

Within Grass's own work the book can also be seen as a clear extension of the techniques and themes of *Local Anaesthetic.* It concerns again the interpenetration of daily personal experience and contemporary history, brought into vivid focus through the introduction of the autobiographical element. Again it explores a consciousness (Grass's own, in 1969) in fragments of reflection and memory, proceeding associatively from one topic to another. The method is made clear enough in the opening pages: Grass thinks of the long 'simmering' process it has taken until Heinemann is finally elected after twenty years of the Federal Republic's existence; he then goes on to reflect upon the benefits of patient waiting, and his thoughts then turn to a dish of tripe that has been simmering for four hours (*From the Diary of a Snail*, pp. 7, 12). The slow rate of political progress is associatively linked with recipes for good cooking, and many other processes.

Equally important is the realization in this book of another feature of stream-of-consciousness writing: the representation of simultaneous or superimposed images within the mind. Travelling about Germany from one whistle-stop engagement to another, the routine of everyday life broken by the punishing schedule of events and the moments of complete idleness, Grass's mind wanders to distant times and places: 'For thirty miles I sleep myself back to the Vistula lowlands, across wheatfields and drainage ditches, beside which stand willows making faces; in so doing, I refute the contention that a body can only be in one place at any given moment . . .' (p. 79); 'I have always had a passion for simultaneous events.' (p. 79); this passion is freely indulged in the *Diary* as the political campaign evokes thoughts of the past or of home in Berlin.

As in the case of *Dog Years*, the origin of the technique of juxtaposing simultaneous events is Alfred Döblin again. *From the Diary of a Snail* exhibits once more Grass's profound debt to modernist writers of the earlier twentieth century. The constant halting and interrupting of one strand of narrative by another bears the stamp of the techniques of Brechtian theatre, where various media – music, speech, gesture, stage design – are combined in a deliberately dissonant fashion so as to inhibit the development of deterministic plot-sequence and to promote critical reflection upon the possibility of alternative outcomes. Grass's intention is different, but essentially related and equally deliberate: the cluster of simultaneous events and associations slows down the movement of narrative and prevents any single or simple line of development from emerging. Matters proceed 'at a snail's pace', in order to convey the book's fundamental conception of time and history and progress.

The main focus of the novel is the inter-relation of the day-to-day events of the campaign with the narrative account of the life of Hermann Ott, or 'Doubt', told by Grass to his children in an attempt to justify his absences. That story is presented ambiguously, to blur the prosaic distinctions of fact and fiction. It is in its essentials a 'true' story of some wartime experiences of the notable West German critic Marcel Reich-Ranicki (who is of Polish origin); to complicate matters further, Ranicki is himself a point of reference in the book, as Grass's mind returns to speculate what he would make of this transposed biography. Yet some of its materials, and also the themes of the *Diary* as a whole, stem from another source, an invitation received and accepted during the course of the 1969 campaign to give a lecture on Dürer for the anniversary year of 1971: '. . . . the draft of a lecture, which thanks to Dr Glaser's prepaid time I won't have to deliver for another two years, is expanding into the *Diary of a Snail*.' (p. 12). Ott's nickname 'Doubt', for instance, is derived from the personified figure of Melancholy in Dürer's engraving, and his christian name Hermann is given by Dr Glaser, the official from whom the invitation comes. In modernist fashion, the book lays bare the machinery of its conception and execution, so that from one angle at least it can be approached as a 'documentary' novel providing an immensely detailed account of the circumstances that produce it.

This simultaneous interweaving of multiple narrative strands produces the familiar Grassian 'baroque' wealth of patterns and parallels, relating them and commenting upon each other. A sketch of some is essential in order to bring out the *Diary's* themes. Grass's campaign diary and the narrative of Ott's life mirror each other, the one a 'diary of a snail', the other the story of a man with a passion for snails, who writes a literal record of their habits. Moreover, the two narratives are framed between comparable significant dates that mark apparent endings or beginnings of historical periods: Ott's story stretches from the rise of the Nazis in Danzig in 1933 to the collapse of Danzig in 1945, Grass's story from the election of the first Social Democrat President to the ending of twenty years of Christian Democrat rule. Each protagonist is a sceptic engaging in political activity, Grass in the campaign for the SPD, Ott in the defence of the Jewish community of Danzig; at one level or another both have to seek refuge from this commitment in some secure and enclosed space (the cellar for Ott, the home for Grass) of which the snail's shell is the central symbol. Each has pedagogic, and perhaps pedantic impulses, of which they are both self-ironically aware; they stand for articulacy and rationality, and they encounter tragic inarticulacy (Lisbeth Stomma, Manfred Augst). The parallels are pursued in a prodigal, loose and unsystematic fashion.

The third central term of the patterns of the book is provided by the figure of Melancholy in Dürer's engraving. It stands for Grass at the head of the tradition of German idealism, brooding presciently on the historical disasters to come, providing a sense of the continuity of the intellectual tradition in which both Grass and 'Doubt' are shown to stand. They are linked with her in a variety of ways: historically, for instance, through the common mediation of Schopenhauer, the pessimistic philosopher of Danzig seen both by 'Doubt' (assistant secretary of the Schopenhauer society at the time of the Nazi victory in April 1933) and Grass as a significant mentor, the antithesis of Hegelian idealism. In other more arabesque ways the parallels are reinforced: Dürer's 'Melancholy', like Grass's *Diary*, draws upon the artist's wife for inspiration; the figure wears a crown (probably of watercress in the engraving, for it was thought that 'water on the brain' combated the earth-binding tendencies of melancholy) which is the counterpart of Grass's fame and public significance; the 'black choler' with which she is seized recurs in the form of Grass's political opponents, the CDU, or 'Blacks' as they are popularly known in West Germany because of the party colours. Despite their playfulness, the correspondences provide a perspective from which to judge the slow rate of historical progress from 1514 to 1969. In both years there is a great deal of 'blackness' for Melancholy to despair about.

The famous 'real-life' personalities and politicians who inhabit the diary are woven into this artistically determined set of parallels and correspondences. The most famous of these is Willy Brandt; he is portrayed as a melancholy sceptic in parallel to Grass, Ott, and Dürer's personified abstraction. During the campaign he carries about with him the stop-watch of August Bebel, the founder of German social democracy; Grass makes it a symbol of the slow process of reform. In between campaign appearances Brandt retires, like Grass and Ott, 'into his shell', fiddling with matches, anxious and taciturn. He is no heroic leader in the romantic tradition of German idealism, and the crucial victory with which the novel ends is no radical 'fresh start' of a new golden age, but rather a marginal, problematical gain, bringing with it new responsibilities and challenges to face, from which the temptation to withdraw is strong. It is known how intensely these pressures weighed upon Brandt.

Played out against this historical panorama are the apparently trivial dramas of Grass's domestic life, made of such stuff as boredom, petty squabbles and jealousies, inconsistencies and frustrations. In fact, this contrast is apparent rather than real, for the meaning and purpose of reform is tested against the nature of the young generation that is to benefit from them. In the home we see the aggressions and tensions, conflicts of interests and egos that make it impossible to wipe clean the slate of the past and begin a new historic era. A glass of water is spilled at table, as the children grumble over a dish of tripe; no-one wants to fetch a cloth, and so strife breaks out as insults are traded in the shrill Berlin accents of the father rather than the mild Swiss diminutives of the mother (see p. 3). With affectionate humour Grass notes the very unsaintly nature of his children, who with their demands for horses and record-players are very far from forming the nucleus of some radically 'new man.' (The indulgent parents, despite their conviction that an extra record player for Raoul's birthday is extravagant, nonetheless relent in the end, are themselves deficient in ideals and self-consistency – see p. 251). Just like their father, who read voraciously and 'absolutely' as a child (p. 69), the children ask voracious and 'absolute' questions of Grass's narrative concerning 'Doubt', and are disappointed that the answers are so relative and so qualified. They want the 'truth' about the past, not artistic lies and fictions, hard facts and real people rather than speculative models of understanding. When Grass shows the children a postcard reproduction of Dürer's engraving to relieve their Sunday boredom, they are engagingly dismissive of such oblique statements: 'What's wrong with her? Apartment hunting? . . . Maybe she's only art or some such junk.' (p. 103). Some of the domestic scenes in the book are somewhat ponderous and trite, but their purpose – to show how difficult it is to teach anyone anything about the past – carries one of Grass's major themes.

The snail image, one of a line of animal emblems in Grass's work, refers quite unequivocally of course to the slow rate at which children learn, adults alter their habits and historical changes are realized. Upon this premise – that every lasting change takes place slowly – Grass builds an exploration of the virtues of patience and gradualism. Not only in politics is the 'policy of small steps' (Brandt's phrase for the development of the reconciliation with Eastern Europe that was the chief

focus of his Chancellorship) of beneficial effect in Grass's
book; it is also a vital ingredient of the art of narration: 'And
so, if my sentence twists, turns, and only gradually tapers to a
point, don't fidget and don't bite your nails. Hardly anything,
believe me, is more depressing than going straight to the goal.
We have time. Yes, indeed: quite a lot of it.' (p. 12). Moreover,
to be a novelist implies for Grass to be a patient and accurate
observer of people's speech, gestures, habits: patience is one
of the virtues he claims for himself in the autobiographical
section of the book: 'I can listen, not listen, foresee what has
happened, think until it unhappens, and – except when
knotted string or scholastic speculations are being unravelled
– have patience.' (p. 66). Other worthwhile pursuits also
demand a slow and patient approach – making food, for
instance, or making love: 'My advice to you all is not to make
love in a hurry like cats. (That goes for you, too, children,
later on' – p. 72). Once more politics and private experience
are intertwined with laconic irony.

Nonetheless, the book characteristically provides a critical
examination and almost an undermining of its own premises.
Time is shown in an essentially double-edged light; whilst
progress requires a great deal of time in which to work itself
out, the passing of time glosses over the crimes of the past,
enabling those who were implicated to come out of hiding and
resume respectability, tempting others perhaps to embark on
similar adventures again when the memory of the past is
buried. With sharp insight, Grass analyses the Nixonian ploy
of 'toughing-out' the evidence of guilt, hoping that sooner or
later something will come along to obliterate or distract
attention:

> An old trick. Before their crime, criminals calculate how
> long it will take for their crime to be forgotten, overlaid
> by the crimes of other criminals, reduced to marginal
> history. Whether they acted with the pomp of vanity or
> with sickly guile, whether they set themselves up as

giants or whistled a leitmotiv for fate to dance to, whether the criminals bore the name of Hitler or Stalin (whether Ulbricht survived his Stalin or Kiesinger took the seat of his Hitler), time, the passage of time, benefits the criminals; for their victims time does not pass.

(p. 123).

As in *Local Anaesthetic* the television set is the purveyor of a sequence of crimes and disasters that have only a very ephemeral hold upon the attention of the captive audience. On the screen, 'Episode featuring a dog' (an ironic reference to *Local Anaesthetic* itself!) is followed by: 'The bloated bellies of the Ibo children. Dead fish in the Rhine.' (p. 89); when Grass attempts to enlighten his children about Biafra, it's already time for the next programme, 'Bonanza': ' "When it's over, you can tell us some more about Biafra and stuff." ' (p. 90). On the news bulletin, Czechoslovakia gives way to Biafra, Biafra to Northern Ireland, forgotten as soon as relegated from the headlines; the formula of the *Diary*, 'a writer is someone who writes against the passage of time' (p. 124), also means that the writer attempts to challenge the built-in ephemerality and disposability practised by the news media with more solid, less easily assimilable structures of language.

Moreover, the kind of patient application that the achievement of progress seems to require cannot immunize against bouts of depression in which 'melancholy' seeks to escape from time altogether. The tedious succession of one-night stands in different hotels, the perpetual shaking of hands and finding the right catchphrases for the right occasion that make up the portrait of the electoral campaign in the *Diary* provide ample opportunity for melancholy:

> I wish that while shaking hands I could keep both hands in my pockets.
> I wish that just briefly, just for a second, the time it takes

F

to do it and not so long as to attract attention, I could
step behind myself and slip away (hidden by the box-
wood) to one side.
I wish I could refute myself and cancel myself out.
(I wish I could go to the movies.)

(p. 181).

The passage illustrates how Grass refuses to glamorize
political campaigning in *From the Diary of a Snail*. Boredom
infects the routine of campaigning just as much as the routine
of domesticity; Grass's work consistently attempts to erase
the distance between what conventionally is felt to be trivial
and commonplace and what is felt to be historically momentous. The writer keeps his distance from the packaged image
that the politician must exploit, perpetually seeking escape
routes, building a shell.

Playfully through the image of the snail Grass elaborates a
series of images of retreat. Some of them refer jokingly back
to *The Tin Drum*, and Oskar's penchant for hideaways; the
book is full of private jokes about the earlier novels. Other
images exploit the possibilities of punning upon the affectionate Swiss-German term for vagina, 'Schnäggli', 'little
snail': 'more graphic than twat or cunt.' (p. 220). So 'Doubt's'
snail-games with Lisbeth in the cellar have double meaning,
especially when finally her little snail becomes moist: 'On the
forehead of a recumbent woman, who has found her breath
again, the snail rests before she once again finds everything.
(Yes, it's bestial the way she takes him in. "Now!" she cries,
"Now!")' (p. 238). 'Doubt' and Grass both seek to enter the
snailshell as a retreat: 'The two of us practised in the sand:
looking for shelter between widespread legs. (Our hide-in-
the-cellar morality. – p. 150).

Once again Grass's verbal inventiveness links overtly quite
incongruous spheres of experience. The connective link is
supplied by the word '*zwischen*' (between); regularly in the
book sexual intercourse is referred to as the woman taking the

man 'in between'. Stomma sends his daughter Lisbeth to 'Doubt' in order to 'take him in' (between: '*zwischenneh-men*'), and 'Doubt' escapes into reveries of utopia as if he were being 'taken in' ('*zwischengenommen*') by a woman. (pp. 186–7). But the word '*zwischen*' also suggests a poem about the electoral campaign: 'Or write a poem titled "Between." (When in Erlangen I, between myself and . . .)' (p. 162).

In between, in the middle: this is Grass's position in *From the Diary of a Snail*. As in *Local Anaesthetic*, the essential contradictions in reality are registered through the use of oxymoron and paradox; the sexual act is amongst these paradoxes: 'Sometimes I'm sick of being alone and would like to crawl into something soft, warm, and damp, which it would be inadequate to characterize as feminine. How I wear myself out looking for shelter.' (pp. 66–7). Likewise Grass's education: 'I was pretty well badly brought up.' (p. 72). And again the nature of progress: 'standing still in progress'.

From the Diary of a Snail is by no means a flawless piece of writing. It is very uneven, much too self-indulgent at times, much too highly wrought and artificial at others. Yet the nature of the work is such that it can accommodate this imperfection without too much damage; its scrap-book format allows for the introduction of material of very differing quality. The 'rubbish and sweepings' that get taken into this scrap-book act as a kind of guarantee that the work of fiction is not a finished perfect piece of art insulated against reality, but open and generous in its form. Though it is some-times rough and clumsy, the work has warmth and charm in its attempts to link private and political life.

NOTES

1. See especially *One-Dimensional Man* (London: Sphere Books, 1968).
2. See Leonard, p. 69.

BACK TO THE PISSPOT
The Flounder

Grass's next novel *The Flounder* appeared in Germany as *Der Butt* in August 1977 to a much noisier reception than either of its two predecessors. Part of the reason for this was a shrewd promotions campaign by the publisher, which involved the leaking of information and titillation about the novel and its controversial, topical subject, women in history and in contemporary society. Curiosity was aroused to such an extent that the book sold 150,000 copies in its first month, and went on to break all post-war records in Germany for the initial sale of a work of fiction. Critical assessments were more varied, and yet quite a few of the early German reviews were prepared to acclaim the arrival of a new masterpiece. Some (whatever their motive) invoked a comparison with *Ulysses*, and it was pretty generally agreed that *The Flounder*, for better or worse, made a powerful, provocative, immediate impact on the reader, second only to that of *The Tin Drum* amongst Grass's writings.

When the book appeared in Britain and the U.S. in the autumn of 1978, reaction was altogether more subdued, and preponderantly negative. There seem to have been two main areas of complaint: offence at the treatment of the feminist movement, most particularly voiced by women critics, and objection to the book's baroque prolixity of form, which was accused of being confused and otiose.

However, partly because of the conditions under which they labour, reviewers of fiction are notoriously fallible, not least perhaps in their judgement of complexly ironic novels in

158

translation. Grass has repeatedly expressed his surprise at the warmth of international response to previous novels (*Dog Years*, for example) that he regards as essentially German novels addressed to a German post-war audience, and on this occasion it may be that the complex allusiveness of *The Flounder* to German culture, folklore, art and history poses additional problems for its reception abroad. Add to this the novel's deliberate strategy of blasphemy and provocation, familiar in other works of Grass (compare p. 15 above, where Grass underlines the rhetorical function of the 'wicked thief' in satiric writing) but perhaps more aggressively pursued here than ever before, and it is possible to claim that critical reaction to the book in English-speaking countries was short-sighted.

This at any rate is my view, and I believe that as the novel is digested (at an appropriately slow rate) its distinction will gradually be recognized. Far from marking a further decline in his creative output, it displays an undiminished creative vigour. It is the culmination of Grass's recent attempts to write a novel that links contemporary reality with the past, more assured in its form than either *Local Anaesthetic* or *From the Diary of a Snail*, though these three books now begin to assume new relationships, much looser still than those that link the novels of *The Danzig Trilogy*, but making a kind of trilogy of contemporary history. In what follows I attempt to argue this estimate of the book, explaining some of the difficulties that confront the reader and giving an outline account of what constitutes its strength – the fact that it is the funniest novel Grass has yet written.

The basic conception of the book is derived from a widely known fairy tale collected by the Brothers Grimm – 'The Fisherman and his Wife.' The story tells of a fisherman who catches a talking fish: claiming to be a prince, he asks to be put back in the sea. The fisherman freely grants this request, but on his return home to his wife (their cabin is picturesquely described in the Grimm story as a 'pisspot') he is roundly scolded by his wife Ilsebill for failing to secure a bargain in return for his good deed. She orders him to go back to the seashore and demand of the fish a comfortable home in place of the pisspot. The fish fulfills this request, which leads to a succession of others, apologetically presented by the fisherman, and granted without comment: the wife asks in turn for a castle, a king's crown, an emperor's throne, and the papacy itself. Finally she asks to become godlike, whereupon the fish condemns the pair to return to their pisspot for ever.

The main protagonists of *The Flounder* are the equivalents of the three figures in the story: the fisherman, his wife and the talking fish. At the beginning of the novel, the narrator introduces himself and his wife Ilsebill: they are a contemporary West German couple, the wife vigilant about the rights of women. She insists on her priorities in the marriage – sex before narration: she wants a son, and before the novel can start her husband must come to bed. Other demands – a dishwasher, a week in the West Indies away from the kids – stamp her as the updated consumer-economy version of the fisherman's wife.

She conceives, and so the novel begins with a transparently obvious and commodious symbol of fertilization (*Tristram Shandy* is a model for several of its features). Immediate large draughts are taken on this idea: copying the epic boasts of Arthurian literature, the narrator claims eternal life for himself and his wife. The story of the talking fish is an archetype recurring throughout history, its characters constantly reborn. The narrator, like Oskar Matzerath in *The Tin Drum*, is given supranormal powers of memory – though in this novel they stretch back as far as the Stone Age.

The contemporary Ilsebill, then, is simply the latest reincarnation of a series of women descending from the earth-goddess Aua, a late Stone Age matriarch whose three Willendorffian breasts ensured the complete submission and satisfaction of men in the society of her time. During the nine months of her pregnancy, and despite her continual objections, her husband narrates the biographies of an equivalent number of her predecessors who represent stages of the history of women (the figure nine has only surface significance, for the series is really an infinite one, and in practice the narration covers eleven women). These women all inhabit the Grass heartland – the mouth of the Vistula; Aua is metamorphosed into two further rural matriarchs, Wigga and Mestwina, then into a series of Danzig women, the Gothic Dorothea, the Renaissance Margret, the Baroque Agnes, and so on through a series of art-historical terms that ends with a present day cook in a canteen. All the women are cooks, and most of them fulfil other traditional female roles, but from one perspective at least they are all shown to have been directly connected with significant historical events. The fisher-narrator claims to have fulfilled a variety of roles in relation to these women – lover, husband, master, servant, sometimes several of these at once. In the history he relates, as in the Grimm story, there is constant strife between men and women, of a pervasively violent and brutal kind.

The fish is naturally recurrent too. The protean narrator claims that he first caught him in the Stone Age as a subservient male fisherman, ignorant of the significance of fatherhood and its rights. In gratitude for his release the fish tries to educate him; he supports the male side in the struggle against a conservative matriarchy, and remains effectively on the side of progressive cultural and technological forces throughout human history. But latterly he has become thoroughly disillusioned with the results of a progress directed exclusively by men – for one thing, it has made his home in the Baltic and elsewhere almost uninhabitable. And so as the novel opens he has decided to join the women's movement: just prior to Ilsebill's conception, he allows himself to be caught by three lesbians fishing in the Baltic, and offers his services to the feminist cause.

In a kind of negative equivalent of the act of procreation that sets the novel going, the feminists delay accepting this

offer whilst his role in the history of male domination
undergoes thorough investigation. This takes place in a Berlin
cinema where for the nine months of Ilsebill's pregnancy the
fish stands trial (in a tank) before a massed gathering of
progressive women, his testimony providing a second framework for the narrated biographies of women in history.
According to the narrator, who as the author of *The Flounder*
attends these proceedings to gather material for his book,
there would be no novel without the trial and the fish's
evidence.

Essential to the novel's intention is the idea and practice of
an inexhaustible and promiscuous artistic imagination. And
so the history of women which the novel recounts is an
outrageous and hilarious travesty of traditional 'male'
scholarship. The tone is set by a colourful account in the first
month of everyday life in Stone Age Danzig, in which a
pastiche of Lévi-Strauss supplies information for the gaps that
orthodox history and anthropology cannot fill. Stone Age
men and women, it seems, inverted contemporary manners in
classical structuralist style by their habit of eating in private
but coming together for a communal crap; the Stone Age
Prometheus was a woman who stole fire from the heavenly
wolf and carried it in her pocket (hence her name Aua, and
the scar and the itch she has felt ever since); and we also
learn that men first learnt the facts of fatherhood by watching
a woman have sex with an elk and tracing the four-breasted
offspring to this act.

The treatment of recorded history is equally preposterous.
The proposition that male historians have neglected to give
an adequate account of women's role in history draws forth
an elaborate fictional pseudo-history of women. Its categories
are deliberate stereotypes – Gothic women are pale, saintly
and fanatically pious, Renaissance women blasphemous,
Rabelaisian and Gargantuan – which alternate in an
absurdly stylized dialectic designed to mock the Hegelian
Weltgeist riding its way through history. The fictional

biographies are sustained in large measure by their function as parodies, each section creating its own stylistic milieu in the manner of Joyce, perhaps, and each of the women offering excruciating evidence of the continuity of female artistic productivity in the form of bad medieval carols or worse baroque.

Nor is the exploration of the significance of women in the manipulation of historic events conducted in any more solemn way. The fish, who takes the 'hand that holds the ladle rules the world' line seriously for his defence, is clearly satirized, as much as the women, for his jargon and pompous male condescension: the cases he cites are distinguished by their patent implausibility. Thus Margret, the Rabelaisian abbess of a sixteenth century Danzig convent, swears to avenge the death of her father, executed for leading a Protestant revolt against the city fathers; her methods including biting off one man's testicle (and getting pregnant as a result), suffocating another while he's in bed with her and gorging a third on her cooking. Amanda Woyke, the neoclassical, enlightenment Cassubian peasant, becomes a world famous figure through her potato soup, is visited by Frederick the Great and meets up with him again, playing with toy soldiers, when she eventually gets to heaven. And Lena Stubbe, the nineteenth century realist woman, a Social Democrat married to two successive shipworkers who beat her regularly on Friday nights, manages to write a 'Proletarian Cookbook,' gets patronized by August Bebel and travels to the 1913 Zurich congress together with Rosa Luxembourg. In all these instances a great wealth of particular and accurate historical detail surrounds these fabrications, heightening their dissonance and incongruity.

But it would be erroneous to see parody as an end in itself in *The Flounder*. In and through the playfulness a deeply thoughtful exploration of the importance of art as calculated fabrication is mounted. Constantly the fisherman is scolded both by Ilsebill and the women at the trial, who (like the children in *From the Diary of a Snail*) demand an art to document their struggle, full of hard facts, statistics, dates. But, as in *Cat and Mouse*, the narrator discovers that facts provide only fragments of insight; they don't of themselves combine to form any coherent and reliable picture of the past. As in the earlier novels, Grass is here committed to the moral necessity of its recovery; injustices against women, like the realities of Nazi Germany, would sink into oblivion without the effort of constructing their history. But history, unless it confines itself to the collection of fragmentary ephemera, must narrate, and so falsify. Narration is essentially artificial – it selects, combines, arranges details, shapes events and patterns them against each other in order to create a coherent structure. History, for Grass, is vitally dependent on the techniques of fiction.

Even more important perhaps in *The Flounder* is the dynamic role given to calculated indirection as a means of reaching the truth of things. Truth for Grass is always a multiple, never a single idea: the Stone Age matriarchs are totalitarians attempting to suppress the pursuit of truth when they forbid anyone counting past the number three. They are also hostile to art, which is associated at the beginning of history with progress: it is through deceit and subterfuge that men learn to catch more, bigger fish, constructing snares, making better fishhooks '*aus dem Lügenbein der Sumpfvögel.*' Fictions are catalysts of further fictions, with the potentiality of a dialectical transformation of continuity into progress. Throughout history women tell their stories as they prepare potato soup: the peelings are the continuous thread of the narrative they create.

So it will come as no surprise that Grass invents in this novel an antithetical version of the Grimm archetype. Following Lévi-Strauss again, it is a mirror-version which the Brothers Grimm are said to have suppressed when the two variants were first transmitted to them. In the lost version all the terms are inverted: Ilsebill is meek and traditionally feminine, not in the least shrewish: it is the fisherman who has immortal longings, and who restlessly transforms the face of the earth in his Faustian urge to dominate nature. In the end, he seeks to reach the stars, but the fish calls him back to his pisspot, whereupon the Ice Age returns. When she is asked which version is the correct one, the peasant woman who supplies the stories replies 'the one and the other together.'

And so in exploring the roles of men and women the novel takes as a premise the existence of antithetical truths about the matter. From one perspective it gives unequivocal endorsement to the 'original' version of the Grimm story, which is clearly a parable of the disasters resulting from the masculine domination of history. The biographies of the women expose a record of male violence that gets worse as history develops. The men are constantly concerned in the production of armaments – Dorothea's husband is a sword-maker, Margret's father a smith, Lena Stubbe's two husbands work in a shipbuilding factory: their weapons get nastier and their behaviour sicker. Agnes is raped by a Swedish soldier at the age of thirteen; she is permanently half-witted as a result, and this in turn means that she is suspected of witchcraft and thus burnt to death as an old woman. Amanda Woyke's husband beats his three daughters to pulp before departing to join the army of Frederick the Great in the Seven Years War: his work is completed by wartime starvation. Lena Stubbe's fate is equally grim: following the regular beatings of her married years (both husbands then get killed in the war) she is bludgeoned to death at the age of ninety-three in Stutthof concentration camp. The lesbian Sibylle Miehlau is gang-raped and then murdered by a gang of rockers when she offends their masculinity on Father's Day by poking her bare behind at them: they run their motorbikes over her body.

In analysing these incidents the novel explores the feminist hypothesis of a deep psychic disorder underlying the masculine role in history. History itself, such an argument runs, is essentially neurotic, the expression of a search for substitute satisfactions to assuage a deep rooted malaise. The basic male trauma is the ejection from the womb; unlike women, they cannot themselves bear children as a compensation. They are forced to seek substitute satisfactions, sublimating their creativity; forever unsatisfied, they dream of an unattainable reunification with the mother, and pursue historical chimerae.

Grass's characteristic womb images recur *en masse* in this novel. In the beginning of history there is paradise: Aua, with her three breasts, simply gives suck whenever required, and men do not have a conception of dissatisfaction. She is a cornucopia of undifferentiated bliss – even Wigga, the second member in the series, lacking a full complement of breasts, has to supplement the diet of the men with an *Ersatz* drug made from a magic mushroom. From this point onwards, the psychic life of men is obsessed with the image of a lost paradise. The idea of a small, contained world not subject to the process of temporal change – the idea of Danzig or Cassubia or the grandmother's skirts – is polarized against a frightened apprehension of the real world of change and differentiation as something open and unstructured and therefore dangerous. Sexuality becomes a perpetually unsatisfied search for the womb, violence the expression of frustrated rage at its failure. As one of the brilliant parodic maxims in the novel formulates the idea, 'killing is the continuation of sexuality through other means,' war the consequence of a primary sexual trauma.

But the novel gives this set of propositions no more than conditional assent. For one thing, if it is to apply at all, it must apply to women as well as men. Right from the start, when the fish's offer of support involves the consulting of a ridiculous and cumbersome bureaucracy, the behaviour of the feminist radicals is frequently no more than a parodic imitation of masculine styles. The lesbians too look for substitute satisfactions: they are enchanted by a plastic device that enables them to unzip their jeans and stand with legs apart to piss against a tree (cost 19.80 Dm). In the grim 'Father's Day' chapter Sibylle is raped not only by the rockers but also by her three lesbian friends, their fetish the dildo rather than the motor-bike. Woman's inhumanity to woman is just as pronounced as its masculine equivalent – when they discover Sibylle's dead body they run away and make an anonymous phone-call to the police.

So it is hardly surprising that the release of the fish at the end of the novel takes place under a hail of stones from protesting feminist extremists. The novel cannot find, in the attitudes of the radical feminists, a convincing alternative to the male-dominated past. They are imprisoned in a sterile, undialectical polarization of roles which corrodes their conception of liberation. The official, discredited version of the Grimm story with its satiric caricature of the female shrew has its applicability to the novel after all.

Perhaps the most important thing to stress about *The Flounder* is that it is not finally concerned to establish any external or abstract description of the problem of the sexes at all. Its ambition is rather to convert the negative, destructive conflicts resulting from the polarization of male and female roles into a positive dialectic of men and women by embodying within itself a model of how such a dialectic might operate. In other words, it is time to shift attention from the novel's content to its form.

The structure of *The Flounder* embodies a principle central to Grass's concept of art – the idea of the resistance of the material to the process of artistic shaping. Following the aesthetic stated classically by Brecht, its form is discontinuous: no style and no narrative logic is allowed to attain authoritative status. Poems punctuate and comment on the separate scenes of the novel, isolating them from each other. Styles alternate and undermine each other, the characteristic baroque sentences of Grass challenged by a spare, terse diary style. Above all, the material of the present, public and private, constantly intrudes: the narrative must digest into itself the contingent, unfinished experience of daily living.

It is Ilsebill who, within the novel, sustains this resistance.

The biographies of the women are narrated against her refusal to fill the role of '*das ewig Weibliche*', her constant critical skepsis and insistence upon the concerns of the present. It is she who prevents those women becoming mere parodies, and so referential merely in terms of other art: her determination (and that of the other contemporary feminists) to interpret those stories in terms of their meaning here and now gives them the capacity to move us. Humorously and indirectly, as the dedication and conclusion imply, the novel is a celebration of Ilsebill's obstinacy.

The function of the narrative 'I' can be approached in a similar way. Its immediately established protean exuberance is a provocation – put crudely, it is designed to come across at one level as a giant male chauvinist ego. Inevitably it elicits multiple feminist challenges: it masks a fundamental insecurity, it proclaims a desire to dominate. Again these objections are seen as the path to psychic freedom. Once more it is an existentialist novel, in which Grass 'puts himself in question' as he attempts to reply to the feminists. In order to become itself, the self must be able to undermine and lose itself – as it does for instance when the reality of the slums of Calcutta confronts the smiling narrative persona of Grass as Vasco da Gama. At such points everything in the novel (including its subject-matter: should it be about the Third World rather than about women?) is questioned.

I am describing a model rather than proclaiming an unqualified success. The relation of the novel as a work of art to the novel as a contribution to a debate remains problematic and sometimes unsatisfactory. This is a far more assured work than *From the Diary of a Snail*, but its artistic skill entails loss as well as gain. At the end one still may conclude that the narrative 'I' holds too many of the cards and too often merely condescends to Ilsebill's dynamic objections. It is a marvellous narrative device, but a less omnipotent central voice might have given a sharper focus to the dialectic of men and women in the novel.

Nevertheless, at the point at which one begins to criticize Grass in this book he has already outdistanced almost all of his contemporaries by a long way. The extraordinary achievement of creating a kind of metafiction that does not get lost in a hall of sollipsistic aesthetic mirrors but comes out of its labyrinthine patterns still able to address itself with deep penetration to living human issues without sacrifice of artistic integrity is itself a momentous contribution to the cultural predicament in which we find ourselves. In *The Flounder* the novel, as a historical form, is very far from being dead; it may not be at ease with its continuing existence but its state of unrest is self-evidently a creative one. This of itself is a kind of refutation of the pessimistic view that a neurotic race of creatures projecting its unhappiness onto surrounding time and space should, and shortly will, close its account. The return to the pisspot may perhaps be a while off yet.

GRASS'S BAROQUE SYMPOSIUM
Das Treffen in Telgte

When *Cat and Mouse* appeared in 1961 less than two years after *The Tin Drum*, the 'matter of Danzig' had quickly generated another shorter, obviously related fiction. Similarly in 1979 Günter Grass's new book *Das Treffen in Telgte* (The Meeting in Telgte, 1979) is clearly a by-product of his previous long novel *The Flounder*. It recalls in particular Chapter Four of this novel: the story of Martin Opitz, the father of modern German verse, and his part in the Thirty Years War. Writing from the perspective of the present, the quasi-omniscient narrator of *Das Treffen in Telgte* is also given powers of total recall which enable him to relate the pseudo-historical events of a meeting of writers that takes place during the Thirty Years War, and at which he claims to have been present. Grass's style, though possibly more considered and restrained than in the longer work, is again parodistic, developing amusingly grotesque, scurrilous and self-evidently anachronistic incidents of a kind that have secured for the book, if not the fabulous commercial success of *The Flounder*, then at least a long run at number two in the German bestseller charts.

Yet the book differs from its predecessor in its topical, public, occasional dimension. It is dedicated to Hans Werner Richter, the writer who founded and presided over the 'Gruppe 47' during the twenty years of its existence from 1947 to 1967, and who is an essential figure in the notable renaissance of German literature in the post-war period. In its first paragraph *Das Treffen in Telgte* announces itself as a kind of

170

one man *Festschrift* for the celebration of Richter's seventieth birthday in November 1978. The meeting described in the novel as taking place in 1647, is in fact a fairly transparently disguised 'Gruppe 47' meeting, of the kind which Grass first attended in 1955. He has recorded his indebtedness to these meetings on a number of occasions, praising their atmosphere, in which critical yet tolerant discussion flourished; the book, then, is a critical yet appreciative reflection upon the significance of these meetings for the health of German culture. At the same time it offers, for German readers at least, the attractions and hazards of a *roman à clef*, for its seventeenth century protagonists are also portraits of contemporary writers and critics – Simon Dach is Richter, for instance, Andreas Gryphius may be Böll, and the young Grimmelshausen, not yet established as a writer, is certainly Günter Grass himself.

The writers meet in a time of war, their country torn apart by political and religious strife and cruelly plundered by succeeding armies of invasion. Their meeting almost fails to take place at all, for the inn reserved by Simon Dach as their convenor has been requisitioned by Swedish troops attending the protracted peace negotiations at Osnabrück and Münster. Fortunately the young Grimmelshausen, a man of action as well as of words, remembers his special relationship with the landlady of an inn at Telgte, one Mother Courage (Grass and not Brecht, it seems, being the special favourite of the muse of epic theatre). He succeeds in obtaining rooms for them there by intimidating the occupants into giving up their rooms with a story that the plague is threatening. Some of the protestant delegates baulk at this catholic piece of trickery but the diplomacy of Dach/Richter manages to persuade them to bury this and other hatchets and settle under the 'Dach' (roof) thus provided for them. Mother Courage cannot offer the traditional Grass cooking during their stay, for this is wartime, but meritorious substitute comforts are offered to young and old alike by the maids and the landlady when she is not occupied with Grimmelshausen. Reading of manuscripts and the discussion of more and less riveting theoretical issues – the applicability of classical rules to modern drama and verse, the kind of writing suitable for musical setting, the relative merits of dialect and High German – ensues, punctuated by arrivals and departures. The magisterial composer Heinrich Schütz (Henze?) arrives, looking for an opera libretto, and departs again empty-handed, though not before unmasking a second Grimmelshausen deception. He at last has provided some good red meat and vintage communion wine, to the general satisfaction, at least until it transpires that he has lied about their source – they have been appropriated from Swedish marauders. The collective conscience is deeply wounded, and Grimmelshausen is put on trial (like the flounder in the previous novel). On this occasion, he wins the argument, and he leaves the assembly of writers. The other delegates, after much bickering, manage in the end to unite and issue a sober and dignified communiqué calling for peace. Alas, this document is destroyed when the inn goes up in flames. For once the omniscient narrator knows nothing of the fire's cause, and the story ends with three dots signifiying doubt.

Some familiar themes of Grass's writing are immediately apparent. The diverse groupings, rivalries, convictions and prejudices of the writers, meeting as they are during a war whose tangled skein of beliefs, alliances and vicissitudes is continually underlined, provide another image of Grass's preoccupation with the complex plurality of reality. The battle of praxis and theory is waged again, with the autodidact picaro Grimmelshausen/Grass and the rather paternalistic diplomat Dach/Richter constantly at pains to counter or moderate the hydra-headed theoreticians at the congress, one-eyed, dogmatic, purist and idealist in their approach to reality. Grimmelshausen weighs in with the opposite view – 'according to his criss-cross experience, old folks are often childish and children wise, noble ladies coarse and peasants

refined, and brave heroes of his acquaintance have blas-
phemed even at the hour of their death.' (*Das Treffen in
Telgte* – p. 37) The novel endorses this view of life as it is in
practice: Mother Courage, telling her life story, shows a
deeper sense of narrative art than more polished, sophisticated
practitioners; Gryphius/Böll, writing out a melancholy art
deeply dissatisfied with life, has grown fat and sleek on it.

Most prominently, however, the book explores the theme
of language and its relation to action. Writers, its first page
suggests, are men whose activity is primarily verbal; though
they may earn their living as politicians, administrators,
teachers (the presence of publishers at the conference with
bags of coins instead of fat chequebooks is a pleasant
anachronistic conceit), their practical and literary lives are
kept apart. For Grass, who has frequently criticized the
concept of 'committed writing', this is how things should be;
as Dach/Richter reflects privately and publicly, writers have
an obligation to words as a medium that can transcend
ephemerality, especially when, as in wartime, everything else
is in violent chaos and confusion. On the other hand the story
denounces firmly those for whom verbal art has become a
kind of substitute for life. In the satiric portrait of Philipp von
Zesen, for example, the ghost of Grass's old enemy Heidegger
stirs abroad once more (though it may be that a more recent
bête noire, Lacan, is also implicated). Zesen, out on a
romantic, self-communing twilight walk along the towpath by
the inn at Telgte, spies a flood of corpses in the river, in
particular a pair of lovers with their arms entwined. But they
are not realities for him; instead of provoking horror or
disgust, they become poetic metaphors woven in as comparisons in his romantic novel. The war, in any case, for Zesen is
the consequence of the degeneration of language into
impurity, the precepts of Opitz having been ignored. At the
other end of the spectrum Grimmelshausen punches Mother
Courage in the face when she taunts him for his lack of
education and consequent limitations as a writer; for him, in

some contexts, words give way to rather more direct forms of action.

Whether this kind of presentation of the theme is particularly subtle or illuminating is another matter. Some of the satire of scholars coughing ink is laboured, beaten out on a tired drum; what does it matter that harmless seventeenth century buffers (or mid-twentieth century ones) like to dispute a dactyl or two? Though the book may gain something over *The Flounder* in one or two respects, because of its compression, it also lacks the running dialectic of the strife between the narrator and his wife, the undermining of authoritative perspective, that makes the larger novel a much more searching inquiry of its premises. Of course, the discussions between the writers at Telgte should provide such a dialectic, with counter-positions strongly represented, and they occasionally do; the fine portraits of Schütz the composer, fastidious, too refined for the Grimmelshausen lobby, yet a true artist, or of Gerhardt the hymn-writer, limited, prejudiced, severe, yet with some kind of intact integrity, give some of the debates a genuine open-endedness. Yet the difficulty lies in the book's public, celebratory intention, the tribute to Richter and the now-defunct 'Gruppe 47' functioning rather at cross purposes with the author's desire to suggest the crackle of live discussion. There are uneasy moments when it seems almost like a self-congratulatory monument to the establishment of an Establishment.

At any rate *Das Treffen in Telgte* raises clearly the central problem presented by Grass's career to date: how does the genuinely radical and innovatory artist in our time, once lionized, assimilated and even appropriated by the media, manage to replenish his stock of ideas and artistic resources? The repeated insistence upon the necessity of doubt and tolerance and reasonable broad-mindedness has shown some self-contradictory tendencies, for too long an emphasis can make a stone of the heart, and even hatred of intolerance distorts the features (to travesty Yeats and Brecht respectively). In the nineteenth century a greater, though in many respects comparable novelist, Charles Dickens, darkened his vision and intensified his experiments with fictional technique at the very time when almost everyone else was becoming pacified by the unparalleled prosperity and reforming zeal of mid-Victorian England. Moving in the opposite direction of comic reconciliation with life, in the end offering a celebration of sexual aggression as a principle of progressive momentum, *The Flounder*, with its new techniques of pseudo-myth and pseudo-history, seemed an act of self-renewal, opening up real new possibilities of expression; *Das Treffen in Telgte*, cashing in a little perfunctorily on these, not appearing fully to earn or justify its apparent satisfaction with the *status quo* established by the 'Gruppe 47', throws the issue into some doubt. At least this is a state of mind of which Grass approves.

SELECT BIBLIOGRAPHY

This bibliography's chief aim is to be useful to the student, particularly the undergraduate, and to the general reader. The specialist or scholar will wish to read no further than Section 1, which directs him to fuller bibliographies. Section 2 contains a select list of Grass's writings in German, concentrating on readily available materials and paperback editions. Section 3 contains a select list of available English translations, on the same principles; Section 4, a select list of critical writings about Grass in German; Section 5, a select list of critical writings about Grass in English. Sections 4 and 5 contain only works that I have read and found useful, so a lot of valuable material is inevitably omitted; an asterisk indicates an item that seems to me of special importance or quality. Section 6 is the most miscellaneous and idiosyncratic, consisting of background books, in literature, history, sociology, etc. that I have found useful and relevant to Grass; it indicates the kind of reading that is often most rewarding in relation to a writer as omnivorous and 'interdisciplinary' as this one.

Wherever possible, my page references in the text refer to the Penguin editions.

1. Bibliographical Studies

George Everett, *A Select Bibliography of Günter Grass* (New York: Burt Franklin, 1974). This contains serious omissions, and needs supplementing with: Franz Josef Görtz, 'Kommentierte Auswahl-Bibliographie', *Text und Kritik* 1/1a (October, 1971), pp. 97–113.

A useful short bibliography for English readers is contained in: Irène Leonard, *Günter Grass* (Edinburgh: Oliver & Boyd, 1974).

2. Grass's Writings in German

A. *Novels*

Die Blechtrommel (Neuwied and Darmstadt: Hermann Luchterhand Verlag, 1974), paperback edition. First published 1959. *Katz und Maus* (Neuwied and Darmstadt: Hermann Luchterhand Verlag, 1974), paperback edition. First published 1961. *Hundejahre* (Neuwied and Darmstadt: Hermann Luchterhand Verlag, 1974), paperback edition. First published 1963. *örtlich betäubt* (Frankfurt am Main: Fischer Verlag, 1972), paperback edition. First published 1969. *Aus dem Tagebuch einer Schnecke* (Neuwied and Berlin: Hermann Luchterhand Verlag, 1972). *Der Butt* (Neuwied and Berlin: Hermann Luchterhand Verlag, 1977). *Das Treffen in Telgte* (Neuwied and Berlin: Hermann Luchterhand Verlag, 1979).

B. *Poems*

Gesammelte Gedichte (Neuwied and Berlin: Hermann Luchterhand Verlag, 1971). Contains *Die Vorzüge der Windhühner* (first published 1956), *Gleisdreieck* (first published 1960), and *Ausgefragt* (first published 1967), plus previously uncollected poems.

C. *Plays*

Theaterspiele (Neuwied and Berlin: Hermann Luchterhand Verlag, 1970). Contains *Hochwasser* (first published 1960), *Onkel, Onkel* (first published 1965), *Noch zehn Minuten bis Buffalo* (first published 1959), *Die bösen Köche* (first published 1961), *Die Plebejer proben den Aufstand* (first published 1966), and *Davor* (first published 1969).

178 GÜNTER GRASS

In addition, for English readers of German, two very useful school editions should be mentioned:

Katz und Maus, ed. H. F. Brookes and C. E. Fraenkel (London: Heinemann Educational Books, 1971) and *Die Plebejer proben den Aufstand* (London: Heinemann Educational Books, 1971).

D. *Essays on literature*

Über meinen Lehrer Döblin und andere Vorträge (Berlin: Literarisches Colloquium, 1968).

E. *Political Writings*

Über das Selbstverständliche (Munich: Deutscher Taschenbuch Verlag, 1969) paperback edition. First published 1968. *Briefe über die Grenze. Versuch eines Ost-West-Dialogs* (Hamburg: Christian Wegner Verlag, 1968). *Günter Grass: Dokumente zur politischen Wirkung*, ed. Heinz Ludwig Arnold and Franz Josef Görtz (Munich: Richard Boorberg Verlag, 1971). *Der Bürger und Seine Stimme* (Darmstadt and Neuwied: Hermann Luchterhand Verlag, 1974). *Denkzettel— Politische Reden und Aufsätze 1965–76* (Neuwied and Berlin: Hermann Luchterhand Verlag, 1978).

3. Grass's Writings in English Translation

The translator is Ralph Manheim unless otherwise stated.

A. *Novels*

The Tin Drum (Harmondsworth: Penguin Books, 1965), paperback edition. First published in Great Britain by Secker and Warburg Ltd., 1962, in the U.S. by Harcourt Brace Jovanovich Inc.

Cat and Mouse (Harmondsworth: Penguin Books, 1966), paperback edition. First published in Great Britain by Secker and Warburg Ltd., 1963, in the U.S. by Harcourt Brace Jovanovich Inc.

Dog Years (Harmondsworth: Penguin Books, 1969), paperback edition. First published in Great Britain by Secker and Warburg Ltd., 1965, in the U.S. by Harcourt Brace Jovanovich Inc.

Local Anaesthetic (Harmondsworth: Penguin Books, 1973), paperback edition. First published in Great Britain by Secker and Warburg Ltd., 1969, in the U.S. by Harcourt Brace Jovanovich Inc.

From the Diary of a Snail (Harmondsworth: Penguin Books, 1976), paperback edition. First published in Great Britain by Secker and Warburg Ltd., 1973, in the U.S. by Harcourt Brace Jovanovich Inc.

B. *Poems*

Poems of Günter Grass, tr. Michael Hamburger and Christopher Middleton (Harmondsworth: Penguin Books, 1969). Incorporates *Selected Poems*. First published in Great Britain by Secker and Warburg Ltd., 1966, in the U.S. by Harcourt Brace Jovanovich Inc.

In the Egg and other poems tr. Michael Hamburger and Christopher Middleton. First published in Great Britain by Secker and Warburg Ltd., 1978, in the U.S. by Harcourt Brace Jovanovich Inc.

C. *Plays*

Four Plays (Hardmondsworth: Penguin Books, 1972), paperback edition. First published in Great Britain by Secker and Warburg Ltd., 1968, in the U.S. by Harcourt Brace Jovanovich Inc. Contains *Flood*, *Onkel*, *Onkel*, *Only Ten Minutes to Buffalo*, and *The Wicked Cooks*. *The Wicked Cooks* is translated by A. Leslie Willson.

The Plebeians Rehearse the Uprising (Harmondsworth: Penguin Books, 1972). First published in Great Britain by Secker and Warburg Ltd., 1966, in the U.S. by Harcourt Brace Jovanovich Inc.

180   GÜNTER GRASS

D. *Political Writings*

Speak Out! (London: Secker and Warburg Ltd., 1969),
published in the U.S. by Harcourt Brace Jovanovich Inc.

4. Critical Writings on Grass in German

*Gertrude Cepl-Kaufmann, *Günter Grass: Eine Analyse des
Gesamtwerkes unter dem Aspekt von Literatur und Politik*
(Kronberg/Ts:Scriptor Verlag, 1975). Manfred Durzak,
'Plädoyer für eine Rezeptionsästhetik: Anmerkungen zur
deutschen und amerikanischen Literaturkritik am Beispiel
von Günter Grass's, *örtlich betäubt, Akzente XVIII* (1971),
pp. 487–504. Max Frisch, *Tagebuch* 1966–71 (Frankfurt-am-
Main: Suhrkamp Verlag, 1972), pp. 325–335. *Albrecht
Goetze, *Pression und Deformation. Zehn Thesen zum Roman
'Hundejahre' von Günter Grass* (Göppingen: A. Kümmerle,
1972). Hans Egon Holthusen, 'Der neue Günter Grass.
Deutschland, deine Schnecken', *Welt des Buches* 196
(24/8/72). Heinz Ide, 'Dialektisches Denken im Werk von
Günter Grass', *Studium Generale XXI* (1968). Manfred
Jurgensen, ed. *Grass: Kritik-Thesen-Analysen* (Berne and
Munich: Francke Verlag, 1973). Particularly useful essay by
Rolf Kellerman. *Georg Just, *Darstellung und Appell in der
'Blechtrommel' von Günter Grass. Darstellungsästhetik versus
Wirkungsästhetik.* (Frankfurt am Main: Athenäeum Verlag,
1972). Gerd Loschütz, *Von Buch zu Buch: Günter Grass in der
Kritik* (Neuwied and Berlin, 1968). Amongst many useful essays
are those by Enzensberger, Wiegenstein, Wintzen, Klotz and
Krolow. John Reddick, 'Eine epische Trilogie des Leidens?
'Die Blechtrommel', 'Katz und Maus', 'Hundejahre', *Text und
Kritik* 1/1a (1971), pp. 38–51. Peter Rühmkopf, *Die Jahre,
die ihr kennt* (Reinbek: Rowohlt Verlag, 1972), pp. 106ff. Klaus
Wagenbach, 'Günter Grass', *Schriftsteller der Gegenwart*, ed.
Klaus Nonnenmann (Olten and Freiberg: Walter Verlag,
1963), pp. 128–136. *Theoder Wieser, *Günter Grass* (Neuwied
and Berlin: Hermann Luchterhand Verlag, 1968).

5. Critical Writings on Grass in English, or Translation from German

Wesley Blomster, 'The Documentation of a Novel: Otto Weininger and *Hundejahre* by Günter Grass', *Monatshefte* LXI, pp. 122–138. W. G. Cunliffe, *Günter Grass* (New York Twayne Publishers, 1969). Irene Leonard, *Günter Grass* (Edinburgh: Oliver & Boyd, 1974). *John Reddick, *The 'Danzig Trilogy' of Günter Grass* (London: Secker and Warburg Ltd., 1975). George Steiner, 'A Note on Günter Grass', *Language and Silence* (Harmondsworth: Penguin Books, 1969). *Kurt Lothar Tank, *Günter Grass*, tr. John Conway (New York: Frederick Ungar Publishing Co., 1969). R. Hinton Thomas and W. van der Will, *The German Novel and the Affluent Society* (Manchester: Manchester University Press, 1968). *A Günter Grass Symposium*, A. Leslie Willson, ed. (Austin, Texas and London: University of Texas Press, 1971). Angus Wilson, 'Progress down the Middle', *The Observer* 12/5/74. Norris W. Yates, *Günter Grass. A Critical Essay* (Grand Rapids, Michigan: Erdmans Publishing Co., 1967).

6. Miscellaneous Critical and Background Reading

Hannah Arendt, *Eichmann in Jerusalem: A Report on the Banality of Evil* (New York: The Viking Press, 1965). Mikhail Bakhtin, *Rabelais and his World*, tr. Hélène Iswolsky (Cambridge, Mass: The M.I.T. Press, 1968). Richard Grunberger, *A Social History of the Third Reich* (Harmondsworth: Penguin Books, 1974), in the U.S. by Holt, Rinehart and Winston Inc. Wolfgang Iser, *The Implied Reader* (Baltimore, Md.: Johns Hopkins University Press, 1974). Wolfgang Kayer, *The Grotesque in Art and Literature* (New York: McGraw-Hill Book Company, 1966). Hans Leo Leonhardt, *The Nazi Conquest of Danzig* (Chicago: Chicago University Press, 1942). Reinhard Lettau, ed., *Die Gruppe 47 – Bericht Kritik Polemik* (Neuwied and Berlin: Hermann Luchterhand

Verlag, 1967). Friedrich Lorentz, Adam Fischer, Tadeusz Lehr-Splawinski, *The Cassubian Civilization* (London: Faber and Faber, 1935). Herbert Marcuse, *One-Dimensional Man* (London: Sphere Books, 1968). Ian F. D. Morrow and L. M. Siveking, *The Peace Settlement in the German-Polish Borderlands* (London: Oxford University Press, 1936). Jürgen Neven-DuMont, *After Hitler: Report from a West German City* (Harmondsworth: Penguin Books, 1974).

INDEX

absurd, the, iv, 67, 71, 75, 76, 78, 102, 108, 125
Adenauer, Konrad, 12, 13, 125, 130
Advantages of Windfowl, The (Die Vorzüge der Windhühner) see Günter Grass
Aquinas, St. Thomas, 23
Arendt, Hannah, 43, 59

Bakhtin, Mikhail, v, 28–9, 83–4
Balzac, Honoré de, 57
baroque, 84, 119, 150, 161, 167, 170
Bebel, August, 152, 163
Beckett, Samuel, 108
Beckmann, Max, 14
behaviourism, 57
Benjamin, Walter, 63
Benn, Gottfried, 10, 96
Berg, Alban, 14
Berlin, 6, 10, 13, 17–18, 95, 96, 98, 101, 118, 136
Bernstein, Eduard, 128
Bildungsroman, 13
Bismarck, Otto von, 2, 8, 38
Blut und Boden, 5, 35f., 81, 114
Boccaccio, Giovanni, 15
Böll, Heinrich, 171, 173
Borchert, Wolfgang, *Draussen vor der Tür*, 86
Brandt, Willy, 12, 13, 17, 74, 148, 152, 153
Brecht, Bertolt, iii, 13, 29, 89, 98, 101, 104, 115–20, 126, 131, 149, 167, 171, 174
Büchner, Georg, 129

capitalism, 128, 138, 139, 140
Capote, Truman, 148
Cassubians, 1, 5f., 25, 36, 40, 57, 122, 163, 166
Cat and Mouse (Katz und Maus) see Günter Grass

catholicism, 56–7, 76, 122, 126
Cepl-Kaufmann, Gertrude, iii, 135
Cervantes, Miguel, 15; *Don Quixote*, 59
Chekhov, 108
Christian Democrats (CDU), 13, 130, 151
contingency, iv, 75
Cromwell, Oliver, 129

Dach, Simon, 171ff.
Danzig (Gdansk), 1ff., 20, 22, 39, 48, 67, 81, 86, 98, 131–2, 137, 151, 161, 162, 163
Dickens, Charles, 23, 25, 57, 175; *Bleak House*, 127; *David Copperfield*, 43; *Dombey and Son*, 25; *Our Mutual Friend*, 26–7
Döblin, Alfred, 14, 70ff., 87, 149; *Berlin Alexanderplatz*, 70; *Wallenstein*, 71
Dog Years (Hunde Jahre) see Günter Grass
Dos Passos, John, 71
Dürer, Albrecht, 24, 150; *La Malinconia*, 150ff.
Dutschke, Rudi, 138
Dylan, Bob, 145

Ehrenburg, Ilya, 130
Ehrhard, Ludwig, 14, 133–4
Eichmann, Josef, 42
Enlightenment, the, iv, 8, 124, 144, 163
Eliot, T. S., 14, 93
Enzensberger, Hans Magnus, 1
epic theatre, 115, 120, 171
Esslin, Martin, 110
existentialism, iv, 16, 75, 78, 89
expressionism, 109, 116, 143

fantastic realism, 14, 25, 109

183